FITTED

The Christian Checklist

"Put on the full armor of God . . ."
Ephesians 6:11

Alan Clark

WestBow
PRESS®
A DIVISION OF THOMAS NELSON
& ZONDERVAN

Author photo by Megan Hill.

WestBow Press books may be ordered through booksellers or by contacting:

WestBow Press
A Division of Thomas Nelson & Zondervan
1663 Liberty Drive
Bloomington, IN 47403
www.westbowpress.com
1 (866) 928-1240

ISBN: 978-1-5127-0452-5 (sc)
ISBN: 978-1-5127-0454-9 (hc)
ISBN: 978-1-5127-0453-2 (e)

Library of Congress Control Number: 2015911643

Print information available on the last page.

WestBow Press rev. date: 07/24/2015

Contents

Dedication

This book is dedicated to the four ladies who own my heart: Kim, Kristina, Anastasia, and Tasha. I couldn't imagine life without you.

Acknowledgments

I would like to thank my family, friends, and the people of Gateway Community Church for their support and love. Thanks to my readers (Kim, Leslie, Joanie, and Deb) who gave me great advice and to Jennifer Gingerich and Kim Clark for their awesome editing silks.

Introduction

In the summer of 2010, I declared bankruptcy. I was not financially ruined, but I had nothing left in my emotional and spiritual banks. There were too many battlefields and I was not equipped to fight on more than one front at a time. As the pressures of family, work, and life converged, the perfect storm provided the perfect opportunity for my wife Kim and me to learn about the armor of God. We were in battles that were bigger than our abilities. The battles were also larger than the physical struggles we were engaged in. The battles were for our faith. We were fighting doubt and unholy attitudes. We were fighting internal battles. The spiritual forces of evil in the heavenly realms took advantage of our weaknesses during this time.

In May of 2010, we received a call from God. It was the call to adopt three little girls—sisters—from Siberia, Russia. We had been married for 24 years and spent the last year saving for our twenty-fifth anniversary celebration. We had quite a pot of money because we had two great jobs, only a mortgage for debt, and we did not have any children. We learned early in our marriage that we could not conceive. For years, we mourned the fact that we would never have a big family and we would never have babies. As we moved into our thirties and forties, we adjusted to life without children. I was able throw myself into ministry without the guilt of leaving my kids at night. Kim was able to produce musical productions on a grand scale, which culminated in her conducting a concert in Carnegie Hall. We traveled to Europe with teenagers every other year and led quite a charmed life. We even had the band picked out for our twenty-fifth anniversary party, and we were looking forward to jamming with our friends with the sounds of Chicago and the Commodores in the background.

We no longer had the itch to be parents, when God reminded us of a promise He made to Kim when she was a young bride. Years later, as she sat in a worship service listening to a missionary speaker from Siberia, Kim saw a picture of a little girl in an orphanage, and God told Kim that this was her daughter. Later we found out that this little girl had two sisters in the orphanage. God opened my wife's eyes to see that these were our daughters. She did not share this with me for a couple of days, but started having long conversations with God and spending long nights on the Internet researching Russian adoptions. Our comfortable life was about to be turned upside down.

By the time Kim shared the plan with me, she had worked out most of the details. She laid out pictures of three beautiful young girls, ages six, eight, and ten. This is kind of the way she talked me into the whole marriage thing, so I was willing to listen. She explained the process of Russian adoption, the costs of international travel, and the fact that these were our children. We could either adopt them or move to Siberia to raise them. We went on a weekend trip to Austin, Texas, to consider our options and to pray. Everything pointed to yes. We even went to see a children's movie to get a feel for being parents. *Despicable Me* was playing. The movie was about a man who adopted three little girls. I saw myself as Gru when he fell in love with his children. As I watched the movie and talked to Kim over that weekend, I was quickly falling in love with the idea of being a dad. By the end of our vacation in Texas, we had said yes to God's calling.

In the middle of the excitement of being expectant parents, my mom became sick and was diagnosed with colon cancer. We had recently lost Kim's mom to cancer and the reports on my mom were looking grim. Russian adoptions also took a turn for the worse during the summer of 2010. A number of abuse cases involving Russian children accompanied by the story of a mom who sent her adopted son unaccompanied on a plane back to Russia, put a tremendous strain on Russian/ American relationships. Kim spent the summer researching Russian adoptions and trying to find an agency that would take our case. Every door was closed and no one wanted to get involved. Adoption agencies did not have the resources to reach into the far depths of Siberia where our children were living. They were not willing to risk their reputations on an adoption like this one—too big, too far, and too expensive.

Epic Fail

The perfect storm happened in August. We received a call from my parents to meet them at the doctor's office. My mom's doctor had some news and felt that the family needed to be there. On my way to the doctor's office, I received a phone call from our last hope. An agency that had some influence in Siberia called to let me know that there was no way they could do this adoption. They offered to send pictures of other Russian children who were adoptable in other cities. After that phone call, I walked into an office and listened as a doctor explained the options of fighting colon cancer. My mom sat bravely and listened to the prognosis. Meanwhile, I was fighting two battles at the same time. We had lost our babies and this one phone call had opened up wounds that had been closed since I was 30 years old. I was also losing my mom. I was not equipped to fight these two battles at the same time. I did not have the emotional or spiritual depth needed to carry on and continue to pastor other people with deep spiritual and emotional needs. I was bankrupt.

As our dreams and lives were falling apart, I was too. Everything from doubt to guilt surfaced and I began to fight the anxiety that has plagued me all of my life. I found myself extremely sad at different times during the day. I was depressed. At some point in my struggle, the Lord reminded me of the words of Ephesians 6:12: "For our struggle is not against flesh and blood, but against the rulers, against the authorities, against the powers of this dark world and against the spiritual forces of evil in the heavenly realms." This passage introduces what we call "the armor of God." I had preached these passages years before and had even started writing a book on the passage at one time, but I could not finish a full paragraph. It wasn't the right time. At some point in our struggles, I began to put on the armor on a daily basis. As God taught me how to pray with the armor of God, I realized that I was only using 50 percent or less of the power that was available to me. There were some elements of the armor that were natural for me and readers of this book will probably say the same thing. For instance, the helmet of salvation was never my struggle. I believed that I was a born again Christian and that the sacrifice of Jesus allowed me to access the power of God. On the other hand, there were times where the shield of faith was strong and there were times when I questioned whether God was listening to me; I even doubted whether He cared.

The Real Battle

I was battling more than cancer and the Russian government. I was battling doubt and an ungrateful attitude that threatened to ruin my Christian witness, because I was not wearing the full armor of God. I was going to battle every day and every night but there were chinks in the armor because I was not fully dressed for warfare. As I questioned why God would give me certain gifts and withhold others, I realized that He was not the problem. *I was.* I had attempted to wear the armor of God on top of the defensive system that was natural for me as a member of the human race. All of us have self-serving and destructive attitudes that are incompatible with Christianity. In the course of this book, the reader will see the amazing armor God has provided so that we might defeat the powers of darkness that threaten our Christian witness. This armor is our identity in Christ, our power in Christ, and our rights in the Kingdom of

God. At the same time, we will find areas in our lives that are exposed to the enemy because we have attempted to put on the armor of God without taking off our natural defense systems. Each chapter will look at one piece of the armor, which is ours as followers of Jesus. There are a number of items that will be easy to wear, but readers will also see that there are chinks in their armor because certain items will not fit. We must learn what not to wear in order to walk in the protection God has provided.

Surrender

Over the next year, as we were learning how to pray and how to fight the attitudes that could derails us, God went on radio silence. Kim and I had heard the call to adopt, but that was it. He had put a deep love for our daughters in our hearts. I knelt by the couch in our living room at all hours of the night praying for answers. My prayer was that God would take the burden off of me and give me something easier to do. I really wanted to adopt a highway and get it over with! Every day was filled with more paperwork and heartache. Kim was spending every free moment filling out stacks and stacks of paperwork. We enlisted the help of an independent adoption agency, against the advice of everyone who had ever adopted. We even flew to Siberia in December of 2010. We heard the same disheartening words again from the government offices in Siberia as we camped out at their doorsteps in sub-zero temperatures. Americans could not preselect children and these children were unadoptable. They were too old to be considered. We sat at the orphanage with our daughters in the next room, while the translator explained to us why we could not speak to them. As we flew home from Siberia, we sat in silence. We were devastated. The following months were unbearable, but God was teaching us principles of spiritual warfare and what it meant to be a child of the King of Kings. I was engaged in battles on many fronts, but they were *God's battles*. They were physical as well as spiritual battles and God had provided the armor to fight. As I began to lose some of my human defenses and put on the full armor of God, I began to find tremendous strength against anxiety, depression, doubt, fear, and guilt.

As I began to use the full armor of God in my prayer life, I realized that these timeless truths were my identity in Christ. Each piece of the armor represented who I was as a child of God. God had gone silent, but I believe that He wanted me to go to His written Word and learn these truths. As I put on this armor, the doubt that was killing my faith was defeated. I began to really understand who I was as a follower of Jesus Christ and I was able to fight battles on many different fronts. Each day, when I prayed, I would see another layer of the armor of God and the weak places in my life would be exposed. As I continued to grow, I realized that there was a lack of surrender on my part. As areas of my own life were exposed, I began to remove the selfish attitudes and the entitlements. I began to trust more in God's power and less on my abilities and resources. It took 12 months for the door to open to adopt, but when it did, it was knocked off its hinges. My mom began to improve beyond what the doctors expected and she set her goals on meeting her granddaughters. The battles for our children and my mom were not just being fought in courtrooms and doctors offices. We were fighting on our knees and our God was fighting for us.

In the rest of this book, I will share some of the stories of God's grace during the years that followed, which finally led us to bringing our children home in 2012. I will try to teach the principles that sustained us through the eventual adoption of our girls and the loss of my mom to cancer. My hope is that those who read this book will be inspired to put on God's full armor and take a stand. I pray that people who are struggling with doubt, guilt, depression, and anxiety will learn how to surrender and put on the full armor of God. I also pray that many of you will learn how to walk away from battlefields with other Christians in order to be a more effective warrior and witness. Churches will find unity and strength when they stop fighting one another and get fitted for the real battles against God's enemies.

CHAPTER ONE

Put on the Full Armor of God

"Finally, be strong in the Lord and in his mighty power. Put on the full armor of God, so that you can take your stand against the devil's schemes. For our struggle is not against flesh and blood, but against the rulers, against the authorities, against the powers of this dark world and against the spiritual forces of evil in the heavenly realms. Therefore, put on the full armor of God, so that when the day of evil comes, you may be able to stand your ground, and after you have done everything, to stand. Stand firm then, with the belt of truth buckled around your waist, with the breastplate of righteousness in place, and with your feet fitted with the readiness that comes from the gospel of peace. In addition to all this, take up the shield of faith, with which you can extinguish all the flaming arrows of the evil one. Take the helmet of salvation and sword of the Spirit, which is the word of God.

And pray in the Spirit on all occasions with all kinds of prayers and requests. With this in mind, be alert and always keep on praying for all the saints" (Ephesians 6:10–18).

The armor of God is a collection of truths and attitudes that can obliterate the forces of evil in the heavenly realms. After Peter recognized that Jesus was the Messiah, Jesus responded, "And I tell you that you are Peter, and on this rock I will build my church, and the gates of Hades will not overcome it" (Matthew 16:18). Through Christ, we have been given the power and authority to overcome the powers of darkness. We must look at ourselves and wonder why our prayers seem to be ineffective. We need to take a serious inventory of our own hearts to see why we are not advancing the Kingdom of God.

My faith, or lack of faith, was exposed in 2010. God called Kim and I to do the impossible and adopt three sisters from the other side of the world. Meanwhile, my mom was suffering with colon cancer. Kim became a Christian as a little girl and I began to follow Jesus when I was 20 years old. We had all of the power available to us as Christians yet we seemed to struggle in many ways. I was fighting spiritual battles on too many fronts at the same time. I was often tempted to doubt our calling to adopt and to question God's wisdom. In spite of these doubts, I never questioned God's salvation. I have always believed that my relationship with Christ covers my sins of the past, saves me from myself in the present, and protects me from God's wrath in the future. For some reason, that one is easy for me. I also know how to interpret the Bible and to use God's Word in prayer. As a young Christian, I memorized a lot of Scripture and there are times when I can recall whole chapters of Romans. These truths were easy for me, but salvation and the Bible only represent a small part of the armor that is needed in battles like these. I needed so much more to be able to stand.

What Not to Wear

We cannot put God's armor on top of the egocentric suits we were issued at birth. In order to put on God's armor, we must take off our current attire. If we have been given the truths that overcome the powers of darkness, we must wonder why evil is so prevalent in our lives. We must be wearing the armor incorrectly!

In the following chapters, we will learn what needs to come off in order to be fitted for the full armor of God. The armor will not adjust to our self-righteous outfits. For instance, the belt of truth will not fit if we do not discard the belt of personal perspective, and the breastplate of righteousness will never fit over the vest of personal justification. As I was fighting for our daughters and my mom in prayer, I found myself losing on the battlefields of faith and perspective. I learned that I needed to surrender some items before I could put on God's armor. My failure was not a reflection of the poor quality of God's armor. I had attempted to force God's armor on top of my own selfish defense system that I had received at birth. Each item in the armor of God has a counterpart in our world that is detrimental to our Christian walk and prayer lives. As we shed these counterfeits, we will experience tremendous freedom in our walk with God and in our perspective with other Christians.

The Trouble with Togas

To understand the context of Ephesians 6, it helps to know what was going on at the time of the apostle Paul's writing. The church in Ephesus was full of division—in homes, in the church, and in communities. Paul wrote to the church, asking them to fight for unity and he called them to a higher standard of love. In the last chapter of this great book, Paul summarizes the battle the church was facing. It is a well-known passage of Scripture— one you've probably heard in sermons or Sunday school, but if we can look at this passage with fresh eyes, we can see that it is a great guideline for us even today.

Ephesians 6:10–18a is not only a guidebook for unity, but it is also a great primer for the new Christian wanting to understand the faith. Each piece of the armor that Paul speaks of has practical and theological implications that can help us grow stronger in our faith. They also teach us truths that can help us stand in any battle we face. Some of the items are necessary to understand our identity in Christ, and some of them put hell on high alert.

Paul reminded the church in Ephesus that their struggle was not against flesh and blood. The Ephesians were fighting one another and this was causing them to be ineffective and defeated. This message is true for us today. Christian brothers and sisters, who we see as a threat, are not our problem. Our problems are our own attitudes and spirits of greed, competition, and jealousy. These come from a very dark place and do not belong in our Christian community. In order to fight these attitudes and spirits, we must take off these elements in order to put on God's full armor. Human armor will not stand up to the forces that tear apart churches, families, and communities and God's armor does not fit over it our standard issue clothing. Good will and positive thinking are not enough to restore us and renew our churches. We must surrender to God and be fitted to stand.

We Are Called to Put on God's Armor

Just like the church in Ephesus, you and I have been called to put on the armor of God. We do not need to wear God's armor just to look good or to prove our faith. *We put it on in order to pray effectively.* The armor reminds us of God's truth, heart, love, and justice so that we pray with the proper perspective. With this perspective in mind, our prayers are in step with God's heart. Mountains are moved when we join God's battles instead of enlisting Him in our skirmishes. In putting on the armor of God, we learn what it means to pray "in Jesus' name" because our heart, head, and feet are in alignment with God.

When King David was just a boy, he stood up against the Philistine giant, Goliath. Before the battle, King Saul attempted to place his armor on young David and even put a bronze helmet on his head. The poor kid probably couldn't move under its weight. Besides that, the king's armor wasn't fitted for hand-to-hand fighting and Goliath would have slaughtered David if he couldn't move on the battlefield.

King Saul's armor might have seemed appropriate for the situation, because David was fighting for the king, but it was a bad idea. David had a hard time walking around in Saul's armor. We get the idea that it was very clunky for the shepherd boy to wear. The armor of God isn't tailored to fit us. We are tailored to fit God's armor! We are tailored to wear elements that will put evil forces on notice and send God's enemies running. We wear God's armor because we are joining in God's battles.

God began fighting for our homes, churches, and communities long before we ever did. Jesus has already defeated the forces of evil in the heavenly realms. When we put on all of the gear that He provides, we can have the same victories. We must first realize that the humans in our congregations, homes, and businesses are not the enemy. The enemy is evil in the world of darkness that spreads greed, prejudice, jealousy, and disharmony among humans. Under normal circumstances, we are no match for these powers. If we try to fight God's battles without each piece of His armor carefully fitted to our frame, we are open to defeat. On the other hand, when we are covered in God's full armor, we are strong and we can defeat even the greatest enemies of God.

The armor of God consists of the belt of truth, the breastplate of righteousness, the sandals of readiness, the shield of faith, the helmet of salvation, and the sword of the Spirit. Prayer is the weapon we often overlook in this discussion, but it is the pinnacle of God's armor. When we are wearing the full armor of God we understand our identity and rights, as followers of Jesus and our prayers will be "in His name." We will also have a balance of faith and action that puts feet to our prayers. The armor of God is a brilliant look at the power of the surrendered life and the power of prayer.

Before You Enlist

Jesus told Nicodemus, "You must be born again" (John 3:7). For those of you who are reading this book who have not had a born-again experience, you will have a much better understanding of salvation by studying the armor of God. I hope this will allow you to make the leap toward salvation in Jesus. If you are a struggling Christian, you will be surprised at the clarity that comes from looking at the armor of a warrior. Each piece of the uniform is an aspect of salvation. The full picture of salvation, justification, and sanctification becomes much clearer by using the analogy of a warrior's clothing. These big churchy words are understood through a look at the attire of a warrior two thousand years ago and relating it to ourselves today. The items listed in the armor of God are not available through any other religious system. The freedom, perspective, focus, protection, hope, and access to God are only found in the Christian experience as we uncover the meaning of the cross and the person of Jesus of Nazareth.

Now, let's go to the items of our study in order to become game-changing prayer warriors. There is a suit of armor that fits each one of us. As we discard our natural, self-serving suits, a suit of armor is given to us that will allow us to not only pray more effectively, but also to live in greater freedom as we understand the tremendous gift and power of salvation through Christ.

CHAPTER TWO

The Belt of Truth

"Stand firm then, with the belt of truth buckled around your waist . . ." (Ephesians 6:14).

Paul begins dressing the Christian knight for battle with the belt of truth. It seems odd that a knight preparing to fight for his family and church would put on a belt before anything else, but Paul is not interested in a belt that holds up our pants. He is interested in a belt that empowers us and helps us to focus on prayer and meditation. This piece of armor represents the attitude of a prayer warrior.

What is the belt of truth? Many of us might picture a leather belt or a fashionable woven piece of material, but this belt is something much larger and much grander. The first time I saw a belt like this was on TV. In the 1960s and 70s, boxing was a huge event. Families would miss their regularly scheduled shows like *All in the Family* in order to watch a live fight. Muhammad Ali made it entertaining with his political views and swagger. I watched a number of men hoist a belt bigger than their biceps after going round after round in the ring. Great fighters like Joe Frazier, Muhammad Ali, Leon Spinks, and George Foreman come to mind. As the bloodied champions held up the belt in the air, it glistened with gold and silver. These belts were large, cumbersome, and looked like they weighed a ton. They certainly would not hold your pants up. The belt of truth is also the belt of a champion.

The belt of truth is the trophy from a battle that has already been won. This belt helps us to go into prayer with the right attitude. If we are going to defeat the enemy that destroys our churches, we must go into prayer with a swagger from a battle that Jesus already won. If relationships are going to be healed, we need to go into our prayer room with confidence in what God has done for us.

The belt of truth is also the antidote to the despair that many of us experience on a daily basis. A theology of defeat that surrounds modern Christianity is sometimes confused with the humility that is expected of the followers of Christ. We often focus on our failures and cannot imagine a world where the power of God is stronger than the power of our sins. Essentially we are saying that God is powerful enough to save us in the next world, but the blood of Jesus has no effect in this one. It sounds very humble to admit defeat, and I would be the first to say that there are many times I have been defeated, but celebrating our failures does not scare anyone in the heavenly realms. The key to having pride in our Christian faith is in celebrating the power of the death and resurrection of Jesus instead of focusing on our unfaithfulness.

Standing in the Victory of Christ

I learned how to be a victor during one of the darkest days of my life. Kim and I had visited the Dachau concentration camp in Munich, Germany, many times with a touring musical group. We usually walked through the barracks with the teens and took them to listen to some of the music that the inmates had composed while suffering in this nightmare of a place. For some unknown reason, I decided to venture into the back of the camp to the crematorium. I walked into rooms made for five or six people where thirty to forty people had been crammed, unclothed in order to receive showers. I began to feel a horrible oppression and wanted to leave, but I felt a duty to the people who suffered in that place and I continued to walk through the exhibit. I found myself standing in a huge room that was more like an animal cage. There was a small glass door in the wall where a gas canister could pass through. My anxieties began to take over as I stood there and realized that I was standing where thousands of people had been corralled like cattle and then murdered. It was beyond my wildest imagination that anyone would do this. I began to ask God some hard questions. What kind of a human being would design this kind of place? I always assumed that the chambers were a structure that had been transformed into a death chamber. I was wrong. There was detail and ingenuity in the art of death and murder. There was a process for killing, and many engineers spent a lot of time streamlining the process in order to be efficient. It was disgusting.

As I stood by the body-shaped sliding stretchers inside the huge fire pits that would cremate thousands of bodies, I continued to pray and ask God to give me some understanding. This did not make sense. How could the philosophies of the Germans lead to the total depravation of humans in the name of war or progress? Then, I saw a picture that gave me a tremendous sense of hope. On the wall of the crematorium was a photograph of the liberators—a handful of bruised and wounded American fighters. They were extremely young, yet they were the liberators of Dachau. These 18- and 19-year-old men had stopped one of the worst nightmares in history. At that moment I no longer wanted to run. My desire to flee this nightmare was replaced with a sense of pride. I belonged there. My fellow Americans fought for, and won, the right to end this nightmare. If I were a singer, I would have started singing "God Bless America" right there in the middle of it all. I wanted to stand there all day basking in the defeat of evil. I have never been so proud of my American heritage as I was on that day. These young men paid a tremendous price for victory. I didn't even have to pay admission to this exhibit; I just got the thrill of celebrating the victory. I walked in a defeated man, but I stood in the middle of that exhibit as a champion.

This is like the belt of truth in God's armor. When we wear it around our waists, we have the ability to stand in the victory of Christ even in dark and dreadful places. His victory gives us the confidence to stand strong. We have the right to stand in the presence of God because of Jesus' victory over death and into life. We did not win the victory. He did. We did not pay the ultimate price. He did.

What Not to Wear

In each of the following chapters, we are going to look at things that must be discarded before putting on the armor of God. As we discussed in chapter one, there are items of our own self-righteousness that are incompatible with God's armor. Kim and I used to love watching the show *What Not to Wear* when it first began airing. Kim loved the big reveal in the end, but I loved watching Stacy and Clinton throw everything into the trash. Participants had to discard all of their old clothes in order to have a new wardrobe. In order for us to fit in the uniform that God prepared for us, we are going to have to undress and discard a number of items in our wardrobe. Before we put on the belt of truth, there are some items in our closets that must go in the trash. It's time to clean our closets for prayer.

In my own personal battles I have struggled with the belt of truth. My mind tells me one thing, but the Bible tells me another. As I learned how to pray for our children and for my mom, I did not know where to start. I was trying to make sense out of each situation. I was trying to find some human understanding that made everything right. I was also looking for someone to blame when things did not go right instead of standing on the promises of God. The belt of truth will not fit over these attitudes.

In order to wear the belt of truth, we have to shed some of the practical and sensible items that we have lived with for a long time. It's as if we are wearing a belt of perspective that will not allow us to follow Christ when it does not make sense. Instead of adjusting our lives to accommodate the Word of God, we often attempt to tailor God's Word to fit our lives. The belt of champions, which is the truth of God's victory, is incompatible with our own perspective and personal points of view. The belt of truth calls us to proclaim things that we do not see and to count on things we do not understand.

In the Christian faith, there are a lot of things that do not make sense, but we must stand on God's Word instead of our own understanding. Proverbs 3:5 tells you to "Trust in the Lord with all your heart and lean not on your own understanding." We know this verse—many of us may have learned it in Sunday School as kids—but there are so many things that we do not accept. For instance, many people do not accept that the power of God can make us holy. Many people cannot believe that God calls us saints. We have a hard time believing the things that we cannot understand, and we have a hard time putting our faith in things that we cannot work out in our minds. Our dependence on our own perspective and opinions must go in order to wear the belt of truth. The first item to throw out of our closet is the belt of personal perspective that used to be so comfortable.

The belt of perspective must go first because it keeps us reliant on our own views and understanding. Now, there is nothing wrong with apologetics and the power of reason, but if we are going to stand on something that is immovable, we must first know that there are times when things will be beyond the understanding of human beings. We must say, "I am going to pray with an attitude of accomplishment and this seems to be an unreasonable way to start my conversation with God, but this is the way that Jesus prayed." **Prayer warriors in the Bible did not pray reasonable prayers. They faced insurmountable odds, but they had a perspective based on God's power and not their own**. We must claim the victories that Christ has claimed for us. Instead of praying from a human perspective, we are allowed to pray prayers of faith that are based on God's truths.

Jesus Wore the Belt

Nowhere in the Bible is the belt of truth so evident as in the story of Lazarus being raised from the dead. Mary and Martha send their friend Jesus a message to come and save their brother, Lazarus. In the story, we see that Jesus intentionally takes His time and before He can get there, Lazarus dies. When Jesus finally arrives, He is taken to the grave where Lazarus has been lying for four days. Jesus orders the stone to be removed from Lazarus' grave. Martha reminds Jesus of the odor that will surely be coming from the tomb. It's a great scene as Jesus begins to pray for the resurrection of Lazarus, but it's so much more than that. In the opening of His prayer, Jesus models how to approach the throne of God wearing the belt of truth. He comes to prayer as a victor and as a champion, not as a beggar. He does not come in defeat, but in victory. Jesus doesn't apologize for disturbing his Father and He doesn't make excuses.

John 11:41–42a "So they took away the stone. Then Jesus looked up and said, "Father, I thank you that you have heard me. I knew that you always hear me . . ." These words of Jesus—"you have heard me"—are evidence of the belt of truth. Jesus is holding up the champion's belt of confidence. He is confident in God's love. He is confident in God's goodness and blessing. He stands on what He knows is true. Jesus prays this prayer of confidence and pronounces victory before He calls Lazarus out of the grave.

We need to pray this way. To do this, we must hold fast to certain truths—the "I Knows"—about God. What are these "I knows"?

- I know that He hears me
- I know that He loves me
- I know that He created me
- I know that He is faithful

These are the statements of a victor. There are times when I've said, "I know that You hear me," even though my mind did not believe it. I have felt abandoned by God at times, but I refuse to continue to listen to the despair and perspective that comes so natural for me. I've tossed out my personal perspective.

Job Wore the Belt

Job is another great example of a champion of faith in the midst of a disaster. Even though everything he valued was taken away from him, Job kept his faith in God.. His friends sat with him after he lost his possessions, his children had been killed, and his body was torn apart by disease. Each of his friends had a unique perspective and each one of them pulls philosophy from their own personal experiences in life. They are all comfortably wearing belts of personal perspective. They question Job's faithfulness to God. They question his heart and they question his righteousness. They sit for hours and hours, day after day, and accuse Job because of his losses. Poor Job. If these are your friends, who needs enemies? Job is unmoved. He sheds the belt of human perspective and the feelings of despair and puts on the belt of truth.

In Job 19, we find a man at the bottom of the food chain. Job has suffered physically, emotionally, and socially. He has suffered socially because all of his friends, family, and servants are appalled at the sight and smell of him. He has bad breath! His friends have talked to him until they were out of words and patience. He presented every case that he could. Finally, he gives up. We see a man in complete ruin. He then stands in the middle of the ring and raises the belt of a champion. Since he had already raised the flag of surrender, he did not have the right to raise his own belt of victory. After all, he did not win anything. It's as if he walks into the ring of honor and holds up the truth of God for the entire world to see. He says, "I know that my redeemer lives, and that in the end He will stand on the earth." (Job 19: 25) *Job does not hold up his own belt. He holds up the truths of God.* Just like Jesus, he focuses on the "I knows." These are the words of a champion. They are the words of a prayer warrior. Job returns to the "I know" statements in Job 42:2 and states, "I know that you can do all things; no purpose of yours can be thwarted." Meanwhile, Job was sitting in his own filth for days, wearing nothing but the belt of truth. What an amazing picture.

Paul Wore the Belt

The apostle Paul also gives us the words of a champion as he mentored Timothy. Paul was suffering in a Roman prison. He refused to surrender, and he too stands up and takes up the belt of a champion. In 2 Timothy 1:12 we read, "That is why I am suffering as I am. Yet this is no cause for shame, because I know whom I have believed, and am convinced that He is able to guard what I have entrusted to Him until that day." Paul stood on the "I knows" of God even when he looked defeated. He had reason for despair. You and I are called to pray like Jesus, Job, Paul, and many other examples in the scriptures. We begin our meditation and stretching by declaring what we know about God, God's love, God's righteousness, and God's faithfulness. This is the kind of prayer that moves mountains.

Praying with the Belt of Truth

Once we have discarded our self-righteous perspectives we can place our faith in the power of God. When we put His belt around us, or more appropriately, when God puts His belt on us, we take up the belt of a champion. We stand on the "I know" statements that defeat our enemy.

When I pray for our children, I begin by confessing that I know God's love for our family. I know that He loves our children more than we ever could. I know that He wants only the best for them and that I can trust Him with their lives. I know that He created them. I know that He knows every hair on their heads. There are times when the belt of truth takes the majority of my time in prayer. It is so profound that the "I know" statements can go on forever. In the middle of my struggles I finally decided not to focus on the trials, but to focus on the truths. This is the belt of a champion.

As I pray through the "I know" statements, it's like standing in a boxing ring and holding up the champion's belt. I may have doubts about my child's safety, and I may not trust their ability to make decisions, but I can proclaim the victories of Christ. He made me more than a conqueror and I start my prayers with the things that I know.

This prayer was what got Kim and me through two of the toughest years of our lives. God called us to adopt three beautiful, little girls from Russia. The Russian government told us no—or *nyet* in Russian. We heard no five times over the course of two years. I would wake up at two or three in the morning and see the glow of a cell phone as Kim was pouring over pictures of our girls. The monetary cost was 10 times more than we could ever afford. The physical agony of not being able to hold and protect them was more than we could take. In my eyes, our future was never certain. Even during our first trip to Siberia, I couldn't believe that we would someday be traveling through the Moscow airport with three little girls carrying three suitcases headed for America.

This adoption was too big for us. It was too big for the Russian government. It was too big for the American government. No agency would attempt to pull off this adoption because it was too big, too hard, and they had never seen so many obstacles. Trying to adopt three girls from the coldest inhabited place on earth during a recession in the U.S. and the worst political climate for Russian/American diplomacy was a nightmare. My wife had faith. She quit her job and spent her days going back and forth from state offices to county offices and back again. She informed me that we would be moving to Siberia if our children could not come home. That's when my prayers got serious. I had been to Siberia and I had driven by one of the gulags. When we spent a week there at Christmas we enjoyed unseasonably warm weather as the temperature rose to 20 below zero.

In the middle of some very long nights, as my faith was weak and my heart was breaking for these children, I began to raise the belt of a champion. It started slowly and increased night after night. "I know that You created these girls, and You love them." "I know that You have a plan for our lives and You want to prosper us, bless us, and give us only Your best." As the nights wore on, God taught me to become more and more bold and to stand on everything I knew about Him.

After four harrowing trips through Moscow and into the heart of Siberia, we finally brought our girls home. After spending every last dime given by every person that we knew, our girls were in their beds in our home in Tennessee and fast asleep. I went to shut out the lights in our kitchen and next to the back door were three sets of brand-new shoes. They were lined up perfectly in typical Kim fashion. Kim and I stood and stared at the shoes and burst into tears. They were the tears of champions and not defeat. They were tears of joy and relief, but they were also tears to celebrate God's faithfulness. From a human perspective, we had accomplished what two of the largest governments in the history of man concluded could not be done. Luckily, we had shed our belt of perspective and held up the belt of truth, which our Champion won 2000 years ago.

The belt of truth is much like a Super Bowl ring. When a team wins a Super Bowl, everyone associated with the team gets a ring. The front office staff gets a ring. The practice roster and the support staff all get rings. Some teams award Super Bowl rings to the cheerleaders and everyone who works with the team. It's up to the team to decide how many they order and who gets them, but the fact remains; the players on the field are not the only people who get Super Bowl rings.

This is what I love about the belt of truth. Our Champion, Christ, is the One who won the belt. He is the One who can stand in the ring and hold it up with pride. He is the only One who has unlimited rights to the champion's belt. He defeated death. He conquered prejudice. He faced the ultimate in evil and unfair abuse and came out on the other end as the greatest conqueror and hero. He faced hatred with love and won the ultimate victory. As we fight the battles of our day, we start by putting on the confidence that Christ provides. I love to picture our heavenly Father standing before us, suiting us for battle. We do not put on the belt of truth because of ourselves. It is provided for us. That should make us feel like a champion. Now that God has buckled the belt in place, we begin to pray like Jesus, Job, and Paul:

> I know that You love me
> I know that Your great arms protect my children
> I know that You created me
> I know that You are faithful
> I know that You can do all things
> I know whom I believe in…

CHAPTER THREE

The Breastplate of Righteousness

"Stand firm then, . . . with the breastplate of righteousness in place . . ." (Ephesians 6:14).

In order to pray effectively, we must secure a second piece of armor. In the apostle Paul's urging in Ephesians 6, he first lists the foundation of the uniform—the belt of truth—and then he lists the defensive protection that surrounds our hearts—the breastplate of righteousness. This piece of armor is extremely important. The confidence that we gain from it should always be appreciated. The breastplate of righteousness is not only a protection on our hearts, but it is also a reminder of what Jesus has done for us. As we go into prayer, this piece is a reminder of our rights as Christians—*we can go boldly into God's presence without baggage.* It's a reminder of the rights that we have as citizens of God's kingdom.

In Acts 22, there is a story about the arrest and persecution of the apostle Paul. In this passage, we see the privilege of citizenship and understand the breastplate of righteousness.

Paul travels to Jerusalem where he begins a celebration of successful evangelism among the Gentiles. One day, as Paul was at the temple, some men started a riot and dragged him from the temple to kill him. This alerted the Roman authorities who immediately put on riot gear and headed to the center of town. The commander put a stop to the riot, arrested Paul, and held him with two chains. Paul asked the commander for the right to address the crowd and gave his story to the people of Jerusalem. At the end of his testimony of God's salvation and his commission to share the grace of God with Gentiles, the Jews shouted, "He's not fit to live" (Acts 22:22b). Without a trial and with no due process, the Roman commander ordered his troops to take Paul to the barracks, flog him, and question him to find out what he had done wrong. He was obviously guilty until proven innocent. The soldiers assumed that he did not have any rights.

Then, a few verses later, Paul stops the Roman soldiers in their tracks. As they were stretching him out to receive a beating, he asked one simple question that scared them to death. "Is it legal for you to flog a Roman citizen who hasn't even been found guilty?" (Acts 22:25). They had no problem beating and torturing the Jewish people who lived in Jerusalem, but there would be huge negative repercussions for any soldier who abused a Roman citizen. Many civilizations had given gifts to the world—from the Egyptian contributions in math to the Greek contributions in culture. The Romans had taken the Greek advancements in government and expanded on them. They were champions of personal rights for their citizens and they gave the world a political system with checks and balances. The centurion, who was about to beat Paul, withdrew immediately, knowing that this interrogation was against everything that he stood for. Paul's question changed everything. As a Roman citizen, Paul had rights to due process and anyone who denied these basic rights would be punished. In Acts 22:29 we read, "Those who were about to interrogate him withdrew immediately. The commander himself was alarmed when he realized that he had put Paul, a Roman citizen, in chains." The next day the commander released Paul and began the process of collecting evidence and allowing Paul to face his accusers. Those simple words from the apostle Paul changed everything about his trial. They remind us of some simple rights that are game changers for us when we pray. Instead of being unfairly beaten, he held to the rights that were his. Many Roman men fought for the rights that Paul enjoyed and he was not about to let them down when he had the chance to assert his right as a Roman citizen. In the same way, our Savior died to give us rights to the intimate rooms in God's house. We need to learn how to assert our citizenship in prayer!

The breastplate of righteousness is all about asserting our rights as children of God. Too many of us come into God's presence sheepishly, as if we had to beg God for an audience. It's time that we assert our rights as citizens of the Kingdom of God. Paul has an interesting discussion with the commander about citizenship. In Acts 22:28 the commander states, "I had to pay a lot of money for my citizenship." Paul replies with, "But I was born a citizen." You and I did not pay a big price for our citizenship in God's kingdom, although a large price was paid. We were not born into citizenship in the same way that Paul was born a Roman. When we assert our rights as born-again Christians, we are putting our faith and trust in the sacrifice of Jesus for our sins. Putting on the breastplate of righteousness is like showing your passport. It is a reminder of the rights that we have as followers of Christ.

What Not to Wear

Before we put on the breastplate of righteousness, we must rid ourselves of more self-righteous garments. It's time to clean our closet again.

I'll be the first to admit that I hate being wrong. I had a misunderstanding with our homeowners' association this year. Our association decided to put an automatic dialing system in place, in order to alert the whole community of local emergencies. I filled out the form online, but at the first local emergency, everyone in our neighborhood received a call. Everyone, except for me. I went back online and looked at all of the information I had submitted. I wrote to the managing agency to ask why I was not alerted during a neighborhood emergency. After a few emails, the manager asked for my personal information so that they could submit it online for me. This infuriated me. I can use a computer! I once again went online to see what the problem was and I realized that the problem was with their program. We do not have a home phone so the home phone portion of our information was empty. The automatic dialing system is based on that one piece of information and without it you are left out of the system. I had filled in our cell phones, work phones, and emergency contacts, but without a home phone number, we were susceptible to all of the horrors of suburban living, including the cancellation of the tennis round robin or the changing location of the bridge tournament. Oh the horrors! I sat down to write a nice letter to the managing director of our community to explain to them that I had done *everything* right. I answered every question correctly, and there was no need for anyone else to assist me in filling out forms on the Internet. That's when it hit me. I hate being wrong. This is the attitude of self-righteousness that is incompatible with the breastplate of righteousness. If we are going to assert our rights to an intimate relationship with God, we cannot hold on to our own selfish desire to always be right.

In order to put on the breastplate of righteousness, we must rid ourselves of some of these self-righteous garments that will restrict us. Looking at our first parents and their desire to be right, we can see some of the garments appearing in the very beginning. God instructed Adam, the first man, to be free to eat from the trees in the Garden of Eden. God gave Adam tremendous freedom to enjoy all but one tree in the garden. This forbidden tree was called the tree of the knowledge of good and evil. We find in Genesis 2 that this tree was in the middle of the garden next to the tree of life. In Genesis 3, a serpent challenges Eve, the wife of Adam, and he taunts her until she eats from the forbidden tree. She is attracted to the fruit from this tree. She eats it and then shares some with her husband. When God confronts them about their actions, Adam puts on his deflective T-shirt. He could not stand being wrong, because it was not his fault. He could never admit that any of this was his fault. Adam immediately deflects all of the blame to Eve. He had to be right. In his attempt to defend himself and escape any responsibility, he even blames God for the woman, as if it were God's fault for creating her in the first place. Adam says, "The woman you put here with me—she gave me some fruit from the tree, and I ate it" (Gen. 3:12). This attitude was passed down from generation to generation, and it is prevalent in our day.

None of us like being wrong or to be wronged. All of us hate being accused of being wrong when there is a little bit of innocence on our part. Our art of deflection is not compatible with the breastplate of righteousness. When we put on the righteousness of Christ, we have to take off our own self-righteousness, which includes our art of deflection.

The blouse of comparison is related to the T-shirt of deflection. Most of us understand our own shortcomings and we never claim to be right all of the time. The only thing that gives us consolation is that we are not as wrong as other people we know. Children have a natural tendency to deflect and compare. The conversation is pretty much textbook every time we sit and talk about a failed test or a low score. At the end of the discussion, our children will always drop a few hints about the other children in the class. They are sure to let us know that there are children who did not grow up in Russia who scored worse on the test than they did. They begin playing the comparison game. The bad news is: I'm afraid they might have learned it at home. My desire to be right and my standards of comparison must go, so I can be effective in prayer.

The first time I ran a half marathon was eye opening in respect to my competitive nature and my use of comparison. I was going much faster than I had ever run in practice, and running with 30,000 people was the most invigorating thing I had ever experienced. As we got into miles four through six, I slowed way down and was being passed by waves of people. One group was talking and laughing as if they were enjoying coffee. Another group was enjoying mixed drinks and blew right past me. I was feeling devastated by these groups that were passing me and by the lady pushing four-month-old twins who almost ran over me. Somewhere around mile six, I began to pass people. My wife was standing near the six-mile marker. She snapped a picture of my excitement as I had just passed an eighty-year-old woman. It did not matter to me how old or physically decrepit other people were; I just wanted to be better than someone else. My mental state wasn't right that day. The lack of oxygen to my brain revealed aspects of my personality that were very unappealing—funny, but unappealing.

This blouse of comparison is very unattractive to God and to others. We not only deflect our shortcomings and blame it on others, but we also compare our sins to the sins of other people. Instead of taking responsibility, we become competitive. As Jesus offers us the tremendous gift of the righteousness of God, we must shed those items that protect our own self-righteousness.

Righteousness

Before putting on the breastplate of righteousness, we should have a good understanding of the meaning of the word "righteousness." God defines this word. "God is righteous" means that He is right. God is the standard of rightness and justice. In the same way that the Constitution of the United States is the ultimate standard for justice in our country, God is the eternal standard of right and wrong. He is right, even when He does not line up with our understanding of fairness or equality.

In medieval days and in times of famine, most towns throughout Europe had two poles outside of the city courthouse. These poles were the standard for a loaf of bread. One pole was the standard size of a loaf of bread in good times and the smaller one was the standard size of a loaf of bread in hard times. The local baker could be whipped if his bread did not line up with the standard on the courthouse. People would leave their local bakery and walk through the center of town in order to measure their loaf of bread with the standard. When it comes to right and wrong, God is the standard. We are right when we line up with Him and we are wrong when we do not line up with Him. Our measurement against other people who are better or worse than us does not make us righteous or unrighteous. It simply doesn't matter how we compare to others.

Throughout the Bible, the message is the same: God is the only one who is righteous through and through. There is the account of Noah in Genesis. He was "a righteous man, blameless among the people of his time, and he walked faithfully with God" (Genesis 6:9). There was also the story of Job who was "blameless and upright; he feared God and shunned evil" (Job 1:1). These men were known as righteous men because of their relationship to God, not because of their own righteousness. They lined up with God, but their righteousness would not stand without their walk with God. In our desire to become righteous, we cannot compare ourselves with Noah, Job, Abraham, David, or anyone else in the Old Testament. Our standard of righteousness is Jesus. He is not only our standard of righteousness, but He is also the provider of righteousness.

"God made him who had no sin to be sin for us, so that in him we might become the righteousness of God" (2 Corinthians 5:21). This verse gives us a great understanding of how we can put on the breastplate of righteousness and enjoy being right with God without baggage and guilt. The death of Jesus brings reconciliation with God. Many writers have written books on how this happens and there are great explanations, but the truth that God can inhabit a once polluted heart is a mystery. Reconciliation and God's living inside of us is a wonderful mystery that was hidden in the Old Testament, but revealed in the New. Every denomination has a theory about how this can happen and when it happens. When it does happen, we are then reconciled with God. We are acceptable to God.

Snakes on a Stick

We need to look at some Old Testament mysteries in order to understand how we become righteous through Christ. In the book of Numbers, God provided incredible anti-venom for people who were bitten by venomous snakes. He instructed Moses to sculpt a snake on a stick. Anyone who was bitten by a snake could then look up at the snake on a stick and live (Numbers 21:8). How did this work? Did the actual act of looking upward have an effect on the type of venom they were fighting, or was this a mental trick that gave people hope? None of these things matter. It was God's method of healing for people bitten by these venomous snakes. God could have chosen to have people wash in the Jordan River, or He could have spit in the dirt and wiped it on the snakebite. Looking at a snake on a stick was the method of salvation that God chose at the time. In the same way, Jesus is God's method of salvation from our own self-righteousness. Jesus is God's program, or modus operandi, for bringing salvation and righteousness to us. When we look up to Jesus on the cross for our salvation, our salvation becomes real and we are saved. Why? Because God planned it that way. In so doing, we become the righteousness of God. Jesus said, "And I, when I am lifted up from the earth, will draw all people to myself" (John 12:32).

Righteousness is connected to reconciliation. In reconciliation, we are brought back to a right relationship with God. We are acceptable to God. Every nation has a currency that is accepted in their country, and very few countries will accept currencies from other nations. In the same way that certain currencies are unacceptable in other countries, we are unacceptable in God's kingdom. Reconciliation with God means that we are made acceptable and ready to be used in His Kingdom. That excites me. In spite of my baggage, guilt, and history, I am acceptable to God because I followed His plan for salvation. I looked to Jesus on the cross for reconciliation with God.

The Christian Bill of Rights

Putting on the breastplate of righteousness means that we assert our rights as followers of Christ. In the same way that the apostle Paul alerted the soldier of his Roman citizenship, we put the world on alert when we assert our Christian rights. We are in the middle of a spiritual battle and in this battle we have an enemy. That enemy will try to convince us that we are not good enough, faithful enough, or smart enough to walk into the presence of a holy God. Before we confront our true enemies that are against peace in our hearts, homes, and churches, we must know that we belong in the presence of God because we followed God's plan, Jesus.

The writer of Hebrews understood this as well as anyone in the New Testament. After explaining that we have a great High Priest in heaven who understands our temptations and sympathizes with our weaknesses, he instructs us to walk into God's presence. He says, "Let us then approach the throne of grace with confidence, so that we may receive mercy and find grace to help us in our time of need" (Heb. 4:16). The Old

Testament high priest was the only person allowed to enter into the Holiest Place. The process of entering through the curtain and walking into the Holiest Place took special clothes, sacrifices of animals, and at least 10 washings of the hands and body. The writer of Hebrews celebrated the fact that through the sacrificial blood of Jesus, he had access behind the curtain without the need of more sacrifice, more cleansing, or a special outfit. He could walk into the Holiest Place and not fear the punishment of death for defiling God's home. The breastplate of righteousness reminds us that we have a backstage pass to God's presence. Not only do we not fear defiling God's presence, but we are invited and welcome. We are not visitors. We are family. We can go places that guests are not welcome. We enter the presence of God with confidence knowing that He will help us in our time of need.

Before we go to the battlefield and before we put on the rest of the armor of God, we are called to look back at what Christ has done for us. We will eventually put on the helmet of salvation and look forward into the future, but for now, we put on the breastplate of righteousness. This is God's standard of righteousness that is placed on us through the sacrifice of Jesus. As we take off our self-righteous desires to deflect blame and compare ourselves to others, we are ready to be fitted for the breastplate of righteousness.

Wearing the belt of truth and the breastplate of righteousness will change your prayer life. As we go into prayer with the belt of truth, we recite the things that we know are true in the same way that Jesus, Job, and others in the Bible did. We begin by reminding ourselves of the truths that are not self-evident, but are revealed to us in the Bible. We stand on the truth of God's presence even though we may feel abandoned. We stand on the truth that God hears us, though we don't understand how. In the same way that the first item in the armor prepares us for the battle, the second item prepares us to face the enemy. Yes, I have done unholy things in unholy places with unholy friends. The blood of Jesus has not only covered my unholiness; it has also empowered me. I have a right to go behind the curtain to the holy place of God. I have a right to go behind the scenes. As Kim and I spent two years fighting the spiritual battle of adopting children who were deemed unadoptable, we put on the breastplate of righteousness daily. We boldly went where few men would dare to go. We barged into the presence of God, asserting our rights as citizens of the kingdom of heaven. When memories of our failures brought guilt, we did not try to justify ourselves. When we faced our fears, we refused to comfort ourselves by comparing ourselves to others less fortunate than us. We just marched right into the presence of God wearing the righteousness that Jesus gives to those who love Him. Our enemies who attacked with fear and guilt did not have a chance against the breastplate of righteousness.

CHAPTER FOUR

The Shoes of Readiness

"...With your feet fitted with the readiness that comes from the gospel of peace" (Ephesians 6:15).

The sandals of readiness are a vital piece of the armor of God. *They help us see that, as soldiers of Christ, we are on a life-saving mission instead of a search-and-destroy brigade.* Turmoil in families, churches, and communities seems to be a common thread throughout history. Even the very first family in the Bible experienced war and bloodshed. Cain and Abel became the example of jealousy and hatred that resulted in murder. There have been many times in my career when I have been shocked by conflict in the churches where I have served. It seems to hit me in the gut, because the last thing I ever expect is for someone who says they love Jesus to be filled with jealousy. The sandals we are putting on help us to prepare for inevitable conflict, even among God's people.

Having our feet fitted with readiness means that we refuse to dodge conflict. It means that we are not only prepared to put out fires, but we expect them. This is probably the part of the armor that I have neglected the most, because I despise arguing. I actually enjoy a healthy confrontation where I end up with a lifelong friend, but I do not enjoy watching Christians disagree just for the sake of disagreement. When conflict happens, I am not prepared and I'm often shocked by it.

Ephesians 6:14b has many different translations and is packed with meaning and instruction. The Common English Bible reads, "and put shoes on your feet so that you are ready to spread the good news of peace." There is a basic understanding of this verse and a deeper meaning, and both of them are worth exploring. Once again, we must emphasize the importance of having all of the elements of the armor of God. This element has an essential relationship to all of the others. The belt of truth must be tempered with the sandals of peace. The breastplate of righteousness is ineffective if we are offensive to friends and family who need to be softened to God's grace. We need to be measured for some shoes of peace.

On Your Mark, Get Set ...

This verse reminds me of runners in the starting blocks. Their heads are down, their rumps are in the air, and they are totally prepared for what comes next. No one is surprised at the sounds of a gun, because they are waiting for it. No one asks, "Who is shooting at us?" when the blank gun goes off to signal the start of the race. It is expected. The sandals of readiness are worn to put out the fires of discord, jealousy, and strife. If we are ready to make peace, we are not surprised at discord in the body of Christ. We are constantly listening for the gun to go off. We are listening for trouble. We are not afraid of the conflict that is inevitable when you have an organization made up of more than one human being. I heard a story about a man who was rescued from a deserted island. When he was rescued, he was asked about the three huts found on the island. The man said that one was his home and the other one was his church. When asked about the third, he said, "That's where I used to go to church, but I didn't like the way things were run." It's a funny story, but it illustrates my point. We can't escape conflict.

I have a friend who teaches pre-forgiveness. He knows that people are going to hurt him. He is fully aware that there is going to be conflict and discord in the church and in his life, so he is proactive with forgiveness. He has already forgiven me for anything intentional or unintentional that I might do in the next year that might offend him in any way. I've offered him the same deal. That is what it means to have our feet ready to go. When we are fitted with these shoes, we are in the starting block, ready for the unavoidable conflict that will block the way for the gospel to be shared.

Get Your Boots Ready

Kim and I worked late nights as custodians during college. We would go to school and sleep during the day. One morning, I had just fallen asleep when I heard the sounds of people running and screaming behind our apartment. I threw on a nice pair of tennis shoes and ran out to join the crowd. A brush fire had started behind our apartment complex. This is not odd for summers in Texas, but it was about to get out of hand. Instead of waiting for help, many of us started stepping on the flames, which were not very high at this point. Soon the fire was out—but so were our shoes! I was not wearing proper fire-fighting boots and I was not prepared to fight a fire. I lived in Texas. It was over 100 degrees. In the summer, I should not have been so surprised by fire.

As Christians, we must be aware. Our places of worship are like pressure cookers. The people you and I worship with are bombarded with pressure, disappointment, temptations, and struggles. Expect a fire. You may be needed to put out a fire, so you better get ready. One of the best books I have ever read is *Don't Let the Jerks Get the Best of You* by Paul Meier. It helped me to see that conflict is inevitable and that I have the ability to help people who come across as jerks because life had served them lemons. This is the perspective gained from wearing the sandals of readiness and this portion of the armor of God is so vital to all of the others. The sandals of readiness help us to see that, as soldiers of Christ, we are on a life-saving mission and not a search-and-destroy brigade.

The Forward Brigade

The deeper meaning of Ephesians 6:15 is found in a Greek word study. This reveals a word picture showing us a bigger purpose for having shoes of peace. In the distant past, when a king would visit cities in his kingdom, a team of workers would go before him to prepare the city. We have seen this in the city of Sochi, Russia, for the last seven years. The 2014 Olympic Games were held in Sochi, and the Russian government spent $56 billion in preparation. The infrastructure was fixed. Roads were straightened and paved. Sewer systems and electrical grids were redesigned for the large numbers of humans who would pour into this small coastal city. The "forward" team was given the task of preparing the way for the Olympic games. The forward team, in ancient times, went to a city and prepared it for the visit of a king. They designed roads that would carry the king's brigade and straightened treacherous roads, which would be acceptable for the commoner, yet unfit for a king.

Today, our presidents have the secret service that are the forward brigade. When our president, vice president, or other dignitaries travel overseas or visit an area within our country, this group paves the way. We do not need to straighten roads anymore, because our interstate system is perfectly adequate for commoners and the president. We do, however, need to block all of the exits and entrances to the highway as the president passes through a community. If a dignitary is going through a city, the secret service will be stationed in locations throughout the city as well as on the ground. Their goal is to make sure that leaders are able to pass safely through this area of the country without interference. This takes us deeper in our understanding of our special shoes. We are prepared to bring peace to our portion of the world because a king is coming. Discord, strife, and jealousy in the body of Christ may be acceptable for us mortals, but they are unacceptable when preparing to welcome a king!

As we dig deeper, we have to give credit to our friend John the Baptizer. Isaiah prophesied about the need for a forward brigade for the coming of our Lord. "A voice is calling, 'Clear the way for the LORD in the wilderness; make smooth in the desert a highway for our God'" (Isaiah 40:3, NASB). He believed that a crew needed to prepare for the visit from the King of Kings. The roads were not adequate for such a grand visitor! The present state of our community would not be acceptable when the Lord comes. Christians believe that these are spiritual inroads that needed attention and not the physical roads of Palestine. John the Baptizer did not wear an orange jumpsuit and work on the highway crew. He worked in the hearts of human beings in order to prepare them for God's visitation. In Malachi 3:1a, we can see the same admonition to prepare for a visitation. "Behold, I am going to send My messenger, and he will clear the way before Me . . ." (NASB). We find out by reading the synoptic gospels that John the Baptizer was the one who was predicted in Isaiah and Malachi. Matthew 3:3 is the clearest picture of the forward brigade, "For this is the one referred to by Isaiah the prophet when he said, 'The voice of one crying in the wilderness, 'Make ready the way of the Lord, make His paths straight!'" (NASB). John was the secret service for Jesus, although he was not very secret. He believed that his purpose in life was to lead the way for the King of Kings. His intention was to clear obstacles that might prevent Jesus from having a successful visit.

Crooked Hearts

John did not go to the city street departments. He went to the people who had crooked hearts and mangled lives. He intended to baptize them for their perversions so that they could hear the message that Jesus was presenting. He knew that people covered in guilt and shame would not be as open to the message of Jesus. He also knew that people who were walking away from God would not be able to walk with Jesus. The disciple named Andrew began to follow Jesus. At first glance, we would think that he had a tremendous blind faith. He not only followed Jesus, but he also went and called his brother, Simon, who would be called Peter. Andrew was not blindly following Jesus. His heart had been prepared by John the Baptizer. He was a disciple of John. The mangled roads of his heart had been prepared for Christ's visit. The tangled mess of his life had probably already been submitted to God's grace and mercy. The forward brigade had already visited him and prepared him to receive a visit from Jesus. The highways of his heart had been prepared.

John's message was simple, "Repent, for the kingdom of heaven has come near" (Matthew 3:2 NIV). This sounds like a turn-or-burn message and, in many ways, John was a fiery preacher. Why would thousands of people come to see this man preach such a simple (and maybe even confusing) message? They had to have the same questions that we have. Did John mean that the kingdom of heaven was on its way or that the people of his day were surrounded and they better surrender? Was punishment just around the corner? Maybe the message was like the words to

43

the song: "My boyfriend's back and you're gonna be in trouble." This simple message needs some explaining and I'm sure that John preached lengthy messages that explained his position. In fact, throughout the gospels, we see him teaching in various places, even in prison.

John's goal was to prepare people to receive the simple messages of Jesus, his cousin and Lord. His message referenced thousands of years of history. The message was a fulfillment of the messages of Isaiah, Jeremiah, Malachi, and others. His message was a confirmation of the hope that was prevalent around the time of Christ. Those who had studied Old Testament prophecies, especially Daniel, were calling the Israelites to look up and listen up, for the time of Messiah was near. The prophecies of God's redemption and restoration seemed to point to the time when Jesus lived. The Israelites were more likely to follow the many teachers who were collecting disciples at this time, because they had a heightened sense of awareness and expectation. John confirmed what other scholars were teaching in the temple courts. The kingdom of heaven was near. If he spoke English, John might have said, "You are surrounded; give up!" This sounds like a man taking prisoners of war and that would be a good picture of John's ministry.

In the same way that John the Baptizer was the forward brigade for Christ, we are the ones who prepare others to meet Jesus. As part of the forward brigade, we must be prepared to put out fires. We must be in the starting blocks listening for the gun to go off. Discord is going to happen to those who are on the front lines preparing the way for Christ. This is not an easy or a clean job, so we should expect to have jealousy and strife. Expect to put out the fire as soon it rears its ugly head! Before wearing the sandals of peace, we must make sure that we get rid of a few items in our wardrobe.

What to Give Up

The sandals of peace cannot be worn with our smelly selfish socks. Our selfish socks allow us to be comfortable with our own isolated lives. We justify our attitudes and actions using spiritual phrases like, "God accepts me the way I am," "that is how God made me," or my personal favorite, "this is who I am whether you like it or not." We dig in and create a fortress to protect habits and tempers that will not damn us to hell or steal our salvation, but they prevent others from seeing the gospel of peace. When we turn a blind eye to the messages that we send through our lifestyle and tempers, we create obstacles to reaching those who need us. If we are the forward brigade, we have a mission and that mission must not be compromised. We can set ourselves up as an independent state, but that does not pave the way for the ministry of Christ.

The secret service has been embroiled in a battle for the last few years because of their selfish actions. President Obama was going to the Summit of the Americas in Cartagena, Columbia. The forward team was dispatched months before the conference and secret service agents were spending their days studying maps of the city. They were exploring possible "soft" sections of the city where the president would be vulnerable. They would drive different routes that the president could take to find out which ones allowed easy access and easy exit in case of an emergency. As usual, America's finest were using the latest and greatest tools of their trade during the day. The problems happened at night when they went back to their rooms. The agents used the services of prostitutes in their off duty hours. Many of them have confessed their lack of good judgment, but they also claimed no knowledge of a written code of conduct that prevented them from these extracurricular activities. They were not disciplined for breaking a specific rule; they were disciplined for breaking unwritten principles as representatives of the United States of America. They selfishly compromised the integrity of the forward brigade.

This reminds me of a band director who tells his students before every trip "TSBNAFWAEIN." Every student that has gone on a trip with him has learned this saying, and they can quote it verbatim. It is ingrained into the DNA of the band program and the band boosters, and it has been a tremendously effective way to curtail the extracurricular activities of teenagers. It means, "There Shall Be No Action For Which An Explanation Is Necessary." Secret Service agents and followers of Jesus should have this kind of saying in their arsenal. The agents should have realized what we Christians also need to remember. We represent a kingdom. Our goal is to prepare people for a visitation from Christ. Any temper, lifestyle, or activity that is a roadblock to others is simply a stinky selfish sock. We shouldn't have to have a written code for every misdemeanor. Our lives shouldn't have to be filled with "don't touch this" and "don't do that." We should engage in things that prepare the way for the Lord. Activities and attitudes that are the most beneficial are those things that pave the way for others to see Christ.

Fashion with a Purpose

One of the first principles of fashion that my mother taught me was the principle of matching my belt and my shoes. This is no longer the law of fashionistas, but I knew this as a little boy in 1968. I was a hipster wearing a white belt accompanied by white patent leather shoes. The belt of truth and the sandals of peace are supposed to match. It is fun to express our freedom in Christ, which comes from the belt of truth. I no longer live in guilt. I have thrown away the rearview mirror and realize that I can live a life of freedom because my salvation is based on what Christ has done for me, not on what I have done or neglected to do. In the words of the Italian driver Franco in the 1976 film *Gumball Rally*, "The first-a rule in Italian driving: what's-a behind me is not important." The belt of truth allows me to confess so many "I knows" about God and my salvation. I know that there is no longer any condemnation for me. I know that I have been hidden in Christ. Even writing these words gives me tremendous confidence and pride in what Christ has done for me, in me, and through me. We must match this belt of truth that gives us freedom with a life of public service as part of the advance brigade.

Paul dealt with this life of service many times in the Bible. He said, "But take care that this liberty of yours does not somehow become a stumbling block to the weak" (1 Corinthians 8:9 NASB). Paul is discussing eating meat sacrificed to idols in this chapter. With the belt of truth buckled around our waist, many Christians could eat any meat. After all, there is no other god but the Lord. Therefore, meat that was sacrificed to another god was sacrificed to thin air and does not carry a curse with it. Others would not touch the meat after it had been sacrificed. They believed it carried spiritual powers that would condemn the person who touched it. Some, like myself, would see nothing more than a good meatball sandwich or "a nice MLT where the mutton is sliced really thin." (Thanks, Billy Crystal, for that line from *The Princess Bride*.) We could confess that "I know there is no other God but you," or "I know that nothing can separate me from your love so . . . let's eat!" There is tremendous freedom in wearing the belt of truth around our waists, but it must match our mission. Our belt and shoes must be in sync. Our mission is to prepare the way for Christ in the hearts of others. We must make sure that our freedoms in Christ do not cause others to struggle. After all, the King is coming.

The Mission

I love what Paul writes in 1 Corinthians: "I have become all things to all men, so that I may by all means save some" (9:22b NASB). The apostle Paul was a man on a mission, so every day he put on his gospel shoes. He was like John the Baptizer. He prepared the way for Christ to enter the hearts of people. His life was guided by this mission. He refused to allow anything in his life that might compromise this mission. He was also constantly putting out fires. Paul puts the "readiness that comes from the gospel of peace" on our feet because he understood friendly fire. He spent his life trying to put out the little fires that could compromise the church's mission.

We are surrounded by a lost world that is surrounded by the love of God. In our mission to share this good news, we must be ready to fight fires. In the next chapter, we will discuss the shield of faith, which is able to extinguish the flaming arrows thrown from the enemy. There are also fires thrown from within; and we must be prepared to put them out. As we take on the mission of sharing the good news of God's love we must be prepared to fight for peace.

Get Fitted

This chapter hits home with me because my feet are wacky! My local podiatrist has benefited greatly from my foot problems. When I prepare for a race or when I spend a lot of time walking, I wake up with cramps. I have every malady known to mankind, including plantar fasciitis. Every few years I spend a day making impressions onto moldable plastic so that inserts can be fitted for my running shoes. Without these inserts, my knees turn in, my feet go flat, my pelvis rotates more than Elvis, and every step is painful. I have read books on running and tried to correct my form, but it doesn't matter how I align my ankles and my "chi"—it still hurts. In order for me to be successful, I have to wear custom fitted orthotics.

The same is true as we learn to pray effectively. Our feet have to be fitted with the readiness that comes from the gospel of peace. This does not mean that we are fitted with the gospel of peace. We are fitted with readiness. We are in the blocks waiting for the opportunity to race. We are standing in line on race day with thousands of others, waiting for the opportunity to go. When God fits us for these shoes, we go through our day in expectation. We look for opportunities to remove obstacles. We walk with a mission knowing that we are the forward detail for Christ. We are not surprised when the gun goes off because we were in the blocks waiting.

Many people will tell you that you must be Jesus to the world. That is true, but it is more likely that you will be John the Baptizer to the world around you. It is more likely today that you will need to do something that makes the road to Christ a little easier for someone you know. You will pave the way for the love of God to reach hurting people. Know that there will be problems and you will have to keep a fire extinguisher on hand.

With Vision People Flourish

A church with a mission can overcome these small fires. I have never had a teenager get in trouble on a mission trip. Standing in the trash pits of Monterrey, Mexico, or going house to house with Thanksgiving turkeys in Nashville, a sense of mission seems to squelch other desires in our lives. A sense of mission also helps us to overcome personality differences that would normally separate us. A sense of mission helps us to overcome misunderstandings. Love really does cover a multitude of sins.

These shoes of readiness prepare me to run the right race. I'm not running a marathon in TOMS. I need the correct shoes. As I pray, my prayers become less about trying to fix situations in my life and more about being a missionary to my world. My prayers become less focused on my problems and more focused on God's mission.

Our mission of peace can be seen in many of our soldiers. No one wears shoes of peace better than the US military. I hear stories of our men and women serving in Afghanistan. Every time they are home, they bring pictures of grace and love. I hear stories of army doctors healing the burns of the enemy. I hear stories of soldiers who save the children of their enemies. I hear stories of soldiers playing soccer with children and doctors sharing medicine in the name of peace. The soldiers are on a war mission, but we have wonderful men and women who are helping our reputation in the world one village at a time wearing boots of peace. These actions do not normally make the evening news, but they do make a difference for the next generation in places like Afghanistan.

Praying with the Correct Footwear

So, let's add the shoes to our arsenal. With the belt of truth I can confess: "I know God loves me" and "I know that God hears me." The breastplate of righteousness reminds me that I am walking in the inner sanctuary and I belong there because of Jesus. As I move on to the shoes of peace, I am put into a starting block. I am crouched down and ready to take off at the sound of the gun. With my shoes securely fastened to my feet, I will pray the prayer of St. Francis:

> Lord, make me an instrument of Your peace;
> Where there is hatred, let me sow love;
> Where there is injury, pardon;
> Where there is error, truth;
> Where there is doubt, faith;
> Where there is despair, hope;
> Where there is darkness, light;
> And where there is sadness, joy.

CHAPTER FIVE

The Shield of Faith

"In addition to all this, take up the shield of faith with which you can extinguish all the flaming arrows of the evil one" (Ephesians 6:16).

In battles I've faced over the years, I've struggled with doubt. I do not doubt God's love, mercy, or salvation. I've doubted whether God hears me. I've even doubted God's judgment for me and my family. In the year of God's silence, I doubted whether I was even on His radar. There were many nights where I sat on the floor knocking on my desk trying to gain God's attention. I've always known that God loves me, but I've struggled to trust His heart and to rest in Him. For instance, I'm afraid to pray for patience because it may be followed by times of testing. Very few of us can totally hand over our children to God. We dedicate them instead. We are afraid that our children may be called to serve somewhere unsafe if we completely place them in God's hands. We assume that God works all things together to frustrate us and teach us a lesson, instead of assuming that there is a Being in heaven who searches the earth every day looking for someone to strengthen. *The shield of faith protects me from the lies that keep me from an intimate relationship with God.* I can trust Him. I can trust His judgment and His love.

So, at this point in our armor-fitting, we have prepared to pray wearing the belt of truth, the breastplate of righteousness, and the sandals of readiness. Paul announces the next piece of armor in Ephesians 6:16 which is the shield of faith. In most suits of armor, this is a defensive piece, but Paul sees it as a tremendous offensive weapon—one that can extinguish flaming arrows of the evil one. This shield is able to totally annihilate the fiery darts that are thrown at each one of us who call ourselves followers of Jesus Christ.

The Enemy Has a Blueprint for Our Lives

In order to understand the battle, we need to go back once again to the beginning of this section on spiritual warfare. In Ephesians 6:11, we are called to "stand firm against the schemes of the devil" (NASB). God's enemies are our enemies and just as the Lord has a plan to bring us hope and abundant life, the enemy has a plan for us. His schemes have not changed, and we can use his past maneuvers to show Christians today how to defeat the enemy. An older gentleman in the congregation where I serve has been a tremendous resource in this area. Whenever our church attempts to do something new, my friend will outline the battle that will be coming our way. As we began to raise money for buildings and the church was growing, this seasoned veteran outlined the strategy of the enemy. He showed me which church members would be affected first and how the devil would go after families in leadership. He outlined how he saw the enemy working in other churches when he was a pastor and how the enemy would attack board members and leaders in the church. It was a tremendous blessing to know what was going to happen before it happened. We have been able to warn our leaders and our staff. We are bonded together knowing that our battles are not with one another.

God has given us the Scriptures that show us the story of salvation and serve as a guidebook to the schemes of the enemy. He has given us elder saints in the church who have fought the same battles that you and I fight on a daily basis. They can warn us of the battles we'll face so we do not end up fighting one another. Paul warned the Church in Ephesus that the battles they were fighting were not against one another. Finally, God has given us the shield of faith. In the same way that the belt of truth must be seen as the belt of a champion instead of a fashion accessory, the shield of faith must be seen in the light of ancient warfare.

Ancient and Modern Warfare

Arrows were a nightmare for armies and civilians alike 2,000 years ago. Armies would surround a city and make the sky rain piercing arrows that were made with the latest technology. Soldiers would need a shield large enough to cover their entire body as they crouched down waiting for the barrage of arrows to stop. Any exposed area would be torn apart by the piercing storm of arrows. Any person who was uncovered would be killed. After a few waves of arrows, the nightmare would grow worse as fire would rain down from the sky. Every civilization advanced the technology a little more than the last. The Assyrians, Romans, and Greeks all took steps forward in developing materials like pitch and tar that would burn longer and bows with a slow delivery that did not extinguish the fires. Entire cities could be burned out and the people brought to their knees with these overwhelming weapons of war.

The enemy has overwhelming weapons of warfare that can overpower the Christian who is not prepared to fight. In the story of the sower and the seeds, Jesus shows us the underhanded tactics of the enemy. A man goes out to plant seeds, scattering them on different types of soil. Some of the seeds fell on the road while he was walking and birds ate them. Other seeds fell on rocky places and some fell among thorn bushes. The only seeds that produced a crop were the ones that fell on good soil. When Jesus explains this parable in Matthew 13, he shows the schemes of the enemy. The seeds that were sown by the road and eaten by birds represent those who fall at the hand of the enemy. There are people who hear the teachings of the kingdom of God, but they do not understand it. The enemy snatches the joy out of the hands of the follower of Jesus who may sprint toward Christ but is soon overcome with doubt. Doubt is a fiery dart.

Doubting Darts

The enemy began in the Garden of Eden to sow seeds of doubt in the heart of the first woman. He made her question God's

Word in Genesis 3. He made her question His intentions. After God had told Adam not to eat from the tree in the middle of the garden, the serpent hissed, "For God knows that when you eat from it your eyes will be opened, and you will be like God, knowing good and evil" (Gen. 3:5). His seeds of doubt were fiery darts thrown at poor, unsuspecting Eve. He made her question why God would keep them from eating the tree of the knowledge of good and evil. He led her to question God's heart.

This is a tactic used throughout the Bible story. When the people of God leave Egypt and are encamped at the foot of Mt. Sinai, the enemy once again sows seeds of doubt in their hearts. They had witnessed miracle after miracle in Egypt. They had walked through the sea on dry ground before watching it swallow the mighty Egyptian army. When their leader, Moses, was gone for 40 days and 40 nights, they began to question. Seeds of doubt and fear crept in. Many Jewish scholars see the hand of the enemy in the events that occurred. The Israelites resorted to making an idol in the form of a golden calf. They were convinced that they needed an identity like the other nations. They were convinced that they needed some sort of a mascot that gave them credibility and helped them to relate to the world they lived in. The enemy was alive and well in that Israelite camp as Moses was on the mountain basking in the glow of God's presence. When he came down from the mountain, he realized that they had been duped. In the same way that the enemy put doubts and questions into the mind of Eve, he had sown seeds of doubt into the hearts of the Israelites. The enemy's fiery darts of doubt rained down on God's people.

These fiery darts are seen in the New Testament too. Paul tells his young student Timothy, about two men who are throwing fiery darts at the church. In 2 Timothy 2 we meet Hymenaeus and Philetus. They were sowing seeds of doubt and fear into the life of the church. They were being used by the enemy to tear brothers and sisters apart. They were spreading false teaching about the resurrection from the dead and causing believers to doubt God. In the same way that the serpent sowed seeds of doubt into the heart of Eve, these men sowed seeds of doubt into the early church. The church would question God's heart and intentions and even question God's Word. These men were obviously charismatic teachers who were able to persuade large numbers of individuals. Their teachings were fiery darts thrown at new followers of Christ. They ended up destroying the faith of some of the early believers.

In all of these battles, there is a common thread. The battlefield became human beings against one another. Adam and Eve began to struggle in their relationship, but the real enemy was not a man against a woman. The real enemy was the serpent, who had tricked them. Moses was at odds with his own people and began a tremendous struggle that would steal his energy. His real struggle was not with the people of God, but with the enemy who had sown seeds of doubt into God's people. Timothy was given the task of uniting brothers and sisters in Christ. People were leaving the church and friendships were being torn apart because they were fighting one another. The real enemy was not the brothers and sisters in the church. The Galatian church had an enemy that was tearing them apart, but they fought each other instead of attacking the devil. In Philippians, we meet two ladies who are fighting one another. Paul urges Euodia and Syntyche to stop fighting. I love the words in Philippians 4:2 "live in harmony in the Lord" (NASB). When we sing in harmony, we don't sing the same note, but we are on the same chord.

Shields of Worship

In the summer of 2010, the enemy rained fiery darts on me. My mom elected to have part of her colon removed in order to fight her cancer. This was a very difficult procedure, so I stayed with her at the hospital the night after her surgery. The surgeon assured me that she did not feel any pain, but mom cried out all night. Waves of pain would come over her. I have never felt so helpless in my entire life.

Exhausted and spent, I ended up looking out the window at an empty parking lot at 2:00 in the morning. Since the day I accepted the calling of God to preach the gospel, I've been telling thousands of people about the love, mercy, grace, and joy of Christ. I spent my life up to this time counseling people in pain and loss, and I always kept the company line. "God is good, all the time." After reading the Bible through many times, I simplified the whole message of the Bible as a story of God's holy love. As I stared out the window a depression settled in and I began to question God. I didn't question whether God existed. I had settled that one a long time ago. I questioned God's heart and His motives. I started wondering what He was trying to teach us and why He would choose this method. I started asking what lessons He was forcing on me, as if the only reason for suffering in the world was my education.

When I realized that the enemy was sowing seeds of doubt in me, I took out my shield of faith and began to use it. The shield of faith extinguished every fiery dart that rained down on me. As the enemy tempted me to doubt God's heart, I confessed that even in suffering, we see the holy love of God. I began to whisper prayers of faith and trust in God's motives and God's plans. As everything in my life was on trial, I confessed God's perfect plan was a plan to prosper me and not to harm me. I eventually ended up worshipping in a cold and sterile hospital room. Not only did I douse the weapons of the enemy, but I also showed him that the weapons he was throwing at me were only causing me to praise and worship more. This is the shield of faith at work. In our darkest hours, when we are separated from our support systems, we become targets for attack. These attacks will not be effective, if we send up our missile defense system—the shield of faith.

What Not to Wear

As in other chapters, the shield of faith is incompatible with certain articles of clothing that we normally wear. We must shed a few things in our wardrobe before moving forward. We no longer have to live with our doubts and questions about God's character and motives. We must, however, throw away our flimsy umbrella of entitlement in order to get a grip on the shield of faith.

The umbrella of entitlement is a useless weapon in prayer and the spiritual battles that surround us. The enemy will send his fiery darts right through our attempt at self-governing, no matter how well intentioned we might be. In the spiritual realm, no one cares about my degrees or pedigrees. The umbrella brings with it a number of unattractive weapons that are ineffective against the enemy and offensive in the kingdom. We are called to leave our egos at the doors of the church, no matter how successful we are in the world. Entitlement will cause us to doubt God's heart because we project our evil intentions on Him.

In the very beginning of time, Eve began to question God's heart and God's goodness. She felt entitled to eat from the tree that she had been denied. She believed God was doing something to trick her, instead of trusting in Him and believing in His goodness. The Israelites felt they were entitled to make a golden calf as an idol. In the battles mentioned in Galatians and Philippians, there were congregations filled with members that must have believed that their status in society gave them status in God's kingdom and in the church. This attitude leads to certain defeat and leaves us unprotected against doubt.

One of the most condemning stories in the New Testament takes place in Luke 18. It's the story of two men at prayer, one a Pharisee and the other a tax collector. The Pharisee, a religious leader, and the tax collector ended up at the temple praying at the same hour. The Pharisee looked at the tax collector with disdain. He had an attitude of entitlement because he had listened to his own press for too long. He looked down on the tax collector and confessed his pride in not being like that scoundrel. This kind of attitude is deadly to Christians. When all we can hold on to is our own superiority over other men, the weapons of the enemy will slaughter us. If we adopt the attitude of the Pharisee, we would probably have a hard time trusting God because our motives aren't pure.

The tax collector, on the other hand, cried out for mercy from God. He confessed his state as a sinner and relied on God's grace and mercy as a shield over his life. He was totally dependent on God's mercy and had obviously settled the issue of entitlement. He was taking up the shield of faith, and it would protect him from doubting God's heart. The tax collector, who calls on God's protection, will find security rather than the Pharisee who believes that he deserves protection because of his piety. The shield of faith is an attitude of dependence on God's love, mercy, and grace, instead of a reliance on our own personal abilities. In order for us to deploy this shield, we must shed our umbrella of entitlement.

Taking up the Shield of Faith

In Hebrews 11:6 we read these words: "And without faith, it is impossible to please Him, for he who comes to God must believe that He is, and that He is a rewarder of those who seek Him" (NASB). This is the essence of the shield of faith. We must first settle the question of God's existence. The enemy will shatter the faith of a new believer who puts up tests for God's existence. If we are depending on the results of a house sale, job interview, or love interest, to prove God's existence, we are not wielding the shield of faith. There are a number of people in God's Word who questioned God's direction. In the Bible a man named Gideon put sheepskins (fleeces) on the ground for consecutive nights in order to discern God's direction for his life, but not to question God's motives. During times of struggle and doubt, we have to confess that God exists. His name that He unveiled to the Israelite people means "the God who is, who was, and who will always be." We might not always feel the presence of God and our brains might even question His existence. When my mom was in the hospital and I was praying for answers, I started to surround myself with the truths of God's Word. This is very much like the champion's belt of truth. Instead of asking God for a sign to confirm His existence, I confessed my belief in His love and my trust in His plan. I confessed it until my mind began to fall in line once more.

We need to believe that God exists, but we also need to believe that God rewards those who earnestly seek Him. This is a way of saying that God is good and just. He always does the right thing with pure motives. Many of us do not believe in Karma, but you couldn't tell by our theology. I have to confess that my first reaction to blessings in life is followed by fear of a curse. I have always felt that a tremendous outpouring in my life will be balanced by something bad happening on the other side. This occurs because I project my own feelings and shortcomings on God. I project what I would do if I were God instead of trusting His love.

The message that God taught the Israelites in Jeremiah 29:11 is to trust in His heart and His goodness. "'For I know the plans that I have for you,' declares the Lord, 'plans for welfare and not for calamity, to give you a future and a hope'" (NASB). This was probably a pretty difficult lesson to learn after your home had been burned and you had been taken off to a foreign country. God wanted His people to know that they could trust His heart. They could put their faith in His love. They could believe in, and put their hope in, His grace and mercy.

Praying the Shield of Faith

We put on the shield of faith and we pray. We confess that God exists, and we trust His heart. We confess that no matter what the world looks like today, we will trust in God's mercy and have faith in His love. We put our trust in God's heart and He shields us from the mortars of the enemy. It's amazing how much doubt can be splattered by a good dose of trust in God's love.

As I pick up and put on the shield of faith, I usually say some of the following statements: "Lord, I know that You exist, and I trust that You are good" or "Father, I trust You, and I believe that You desire good for me." It is that simple. You might expand this prayer to include a number of things that you trust about God.

There are times that I am like the dad in Mark 9. He had endured a son who was possessed by evil spirits. A child with special needs, who had tantrums and seizures at different times of the day—every single day—consumed his whole life. He was probably isolated from friends and family, who could not handle this horrible display. When this father asks for Jesus' help, Jesus gives him tremendous hope with the statement, "all things are possible to him who believes" (Mark 9:23 NASB). The father knows that his son's healing is possible. He believes that God loves him and wants to heal him. The Bible doesn't give us all of these details, but we can imply that this man has faith. He's also worn down. Years of disease and failure have exhausted him. His money and his energy had probably all gone to the healing of this son—to no avail. He gives the most wonderful and honest answer in Mark 9:24b: "I do believe; help my unbelief" (NASB). This is the shield of faith: a father with an honest answer who believes that he can put his faith and his lack of faith in God's hands.

There are days where my faith is a 10 on a scale of one to 10 and there are days when I barely scratch the twos and threes. When I'm struggling with the shield of faith, I can honestly approach my Father in heaven, who gives faith as a gift and confess, "I believe; help my unbelief," and He does.

CHAPTER SIX

The Helmet of Salvation

"Take the helmet of salvation . . ." (Ephesians 6:17a).

During the spiritual battles of 2010 and beyond, I was constantly reminding myself of the gift of salvation. When I felt that I could not knock anymore on God's doors and my prayers were not being heard, I went back to the spring of 1985, when I understood salvation for the first time. Salvation was not a concept for me; it was an experience. I was saved from bad attitudes and destructive habits when I finally understood what Christ had done on the cross. My salvation was not just a transaction in heaven, it was an earthly experience that shook out the prejudices in my heart and gave me a new start in life. Even though I doubted God's plan at times, I could never doubt the work of God in me. In one weekend, my apartment went from being party central to a house of prayer. During times of testing, we must remember where we came from. The reason I've struggled so much with suffering, is because I've seen the healing work of God in my own life. I don't know why He allows some to suffer and some to be healed, but I do trust in the power of God to save our hearts as well as our physical bodies. We need the helmet of salvation during times when we cannot see God's hands at work.

Perfect Salvation

The helmet of salvation is the most inspiring piece of equipment to me. To many of us, this is the crown of life and the hope of our future resurrection. It's a perfect headpiece for the warrior who wears the belt of a champion, the breastplate of righteousness, the shoes of peace, and who is protected by the shield of faith. *This helmet of salvation is what gives us the most perspective on our present situation in light of our past sins and our future destiny!*

Some people believe that salvation in Christ saves us from our past. Some believe salvation is in the future, while others believe this is a present-day reality. In fact, it's all of the above. In chapter three, we learned about our rights as members of God's kingdom. We become a part of His kingdom through our faith in Jesus' sacrifice for our sins. It's God's plan, even though we might not understand it. As a person who struggles with guilt, I need the constant reminder that my sins are as far as the east is from the west. I'm a new creation in Christ. I've been given the opportunity to start over again because my past is behind me. The Holy Spirit also gives me the power today to keep me from stumbling into old patterns and destructive habits. Furthermore, in the future, I'll join the saints in heaven and I'll live with Christ forever in the place He has prepared for me.

But I Need It Now

In Acts 16 we learn about the salvation of a Philippian jailer. This is a tremendous story of God's immediate saving grace. It's not just the story of future salvation or salvation from past sin. It's salvation from the Roman sword. In this passage, the jailer is housing two very important inmates: Paul and Silas. A mob in Philippi had attacked these two men after they shut down a fortune-telling racket. They were beaten and handed over to the jailer who tossed them into a secure prison cell and locked their feet into the stocks. They were treated as aggressive criminals, but they began to have a church service.

Imagine the scene. Paul and Silas began to sing and pray. The whole prison was filled with the sounds of worship. Around midnight, an earthquake shook the prison and the chains fell off of every prisoner. The jailer woke up to find the prison doors open and all of his inmates walking around freely. The jailer was about to commit suicide in order to escape the horrible torture he was sure to face. He also may have feared the prisoners who were now free to seek revenge against him and his family. He was afraid of the government. A jailer was responsible for the inmates. If any of them escaped, the head jailer would have to serve out the sentence of the one who got away. Before he could fall on his sword, Paul stopped him. The jailer rushed into Paul and Silas' cell and fell down before them asking, "Sirs, what must I do to be saved?" (Acts16:30 NASB). This is a great story, but I do not believe the jailer was talking about salvation from God's wrath or hell. He wanted to know how to escape the punishment he would face as a failed jailer.

Many of us, like the jailer, need salvation now. We know that we will be saved from God's wrath in the future, but our situation is tough today. Our marriages need saving. Our businesses need saving. Our communities need saving. Too many of us focus on future salvation. We forget that Christ cannot only save us from the past, but His power can also save us from our present self-destructive lives. Paul instructed the jailer to "Believe in the Lord Jesus, and you will be saved, you and your household" (Acts16:31 NASB). This is a beautiful picture of salvation past, present, and future. The jailer was saved from his past sins. He was protected and safe from present punishment. He would also be protected in the future when God's wrath would be poured out on the earth. The jailer and his family found that salvation was not a spiritual matter. It was a physical reality in their lives.

A Modern Disaster

When I was 21 years old, I surrender to the love of Jesus. Jesus saved me from my self-destruction and continues to save me from myself on a daily basis. There have been a number of times when this salvation was a present reality in my life and not just a spiritual reality. After God called us to adopt three girls from Russia, Kim and I headed to Siberia in order to speed up the process in person. We flew into Moscow in the middle of a natural disaster. An ice storm had shut down the whole city. It was the kind of storm that had stopped men like Napoleon and Hitler. In fact, there are monuments outside of Moscow that show where these armies quit. We landed in the first airport just as the water mains were beginning to fail, and, as we were leaving the airport, the lower levels were being flooded. After a few hours in a taxi, we were dropped off at a second airport that had lost all power and where the generators allowed just enough light for us to see the thousands of people who were stranded.

As we fought for a ticket to fly to Siberia, riots were starting in the airport. The food supply was getting very low and we continued to pray for God's protection in this tense atmosphere. We miraculously received a ticket to fly out after eight hours of scratching and clawing in a dark, smoke-filled airport filled with thousands of angry people. Our plane only made it about two hours before we landed in another airport in Siberia in order to wait out a blizzard. Exhausted, we fell asleep across rows of chairs in this second airport in the middle of nowhere. We were awakened by the sound of Russian soldiers strapping on their ammo belts. Scores of soldiers were being sent into Moscow to face the riots happening at the airport we just left. Kim and I woke to find ourselves surrounded by soldiers. We were extremely uncomfortable at this point, but we knew that God was saving us. Yes, He saved us from our sins. Yes, He saved us from His wrath; He also saved us in a dangerous situation. We could feel His protection around us, in spite of the daunting figures that were surrounding us. As the soldiers organized and walked out to their plane in the middle of the blizzard, we sighed a great sigh of relief and praise. We were thankful for

God's present salvation, as well as our heavenly home where we will know final salvation. We weren't ready for that home yet!

The Hope of Salvation

There is also a future reality to salvation. In 1 Thessalonians, Paul gives an abbreviated version of the armor of God that sheds some light on this subject: "But since we are of the day, let us be sober, having put on the breastplate of faith and love, and as a helmet, the hope of salvation" (1 Thess. 5:8 NASB). The helmet represents the hope of salvation in both Ephesians 6 and 1 Thessalonians 5. Paul continues in the next verses of 1 Thessalonians to explain our helmet: "For God has not destined us for wrath, but for obtaining salvation through our Lord Jesus Christ, who died for us, so that whether we are awake or asleep, we may live together with Him" (1 Thess. 5:9–10 NASB). This is the present and future reality of salvation. We walk together with Christ in this world. He saves us daily. He also will save us when our earthly bodies are done. When we die, there is a salvation from death as there is a salvation from self-destruction in this world. There is a present and a future salvation and we see it in this passage. We are with Christ in this world or in the next one.

In the previous chapter of 1 Thessalonians, we find some of the most exciting verses in all of the Scriptures. We see what this hope of salvation will look like: "For the Lord Himself will descend from heaven with a shout, with the voice of the archangel and with the trumpet of God, and the dead in Christ shall rise first.

Then we who are alive and remain shall be caught up together with them in the clouds to meet the Lord in the air, and so we shall always be with the Lord" (1Thess. 4:16-17 NASB). This is our future salvation. It is our reminder that we will not always struggle with these physical bodies. Our future salvation gives perspective to the life we now live.

Perfect Perspective

The helmet of salvation is an integral part of our armor. Each piece so far has given us a unique perspective. The belt of truth reminds us of the victory of Christ over sin. The breastplate of righteousness reminds us of the privilege to be in God's presence. The shoes are a reminder of the peaceful purposes of our battle. The shield of faith reminds us that God is faithful and we should look for His reward. The helmet helps to minimize the physical battles of this world in light of the present and future salvation of our souls.

It's amazing how much time I spend on insignificant issues when I lose perspective. In our family, we have seven guitars. Every child can have a guitar. We all share one pick for some reason, and it drives me crazy that our girls never put the pick back on the guitar. I find our one, precious pick all over the house. If you purchased this book, you helped the cause, because when I sell 100 books, I am going to buy guitar picks for our family.

I also have a Larrivee guitar that is my baby. It's always housed in a case and it only comes out when I want to play a little acoustical jazz. It is one of my prized possessions in life. I have it because my parents, my wife, and our church gave me a large amount of money to buy it. On one ill-fated night, during the summer of 2012, my guitar was in my office at church. The teenagers were about to start worship, but they needed a guitar. They asked to borrow it and I said, "Of course, but be careful." My Larrivee sat on the stage waiting to be played, when a volleyball came flying across the room and hit a microphone stand. The teens all tell me that the incident happened in slow motion. It's one of our church's modern-day tragedies in their minds. The microphone stand slowly descended to the ground and, at the last minute, it scraped across the face of my baby— my beautiful dream guitar.

I wasn't in the room at the time, but I'm told that a silence fell across the room. Everyone wondered who would go and give me the news. My associate pastor, Jason, decide he would take the fall. He came to me with his heart beating out of his chest and his face about to explode. As he gave me the news, I saw teenagers in the background huddled in groups, probably praying and asking for forgiveness for their sins because they were sure that someone was about to pay the price. When I saw Jason's face and noticed the scared teenagers behind him, God gave me a wonderful sense of perspective. The students in the room had eternal souls that had unlimited potential and priceless value. I decided not to go and inspect the guitar. It wasn't important how much of the face had been scratched. The important thing was that we all gained an eternal perspective through the ill fate of my favorite possession. I knew that someday when Christ returned for me, I couldn't take this glorified toothpick with me. At the trumpet call of God, this instrument would become firewood for those who are left behind. At that point, expensive guitars will be worthless. Only human souls will have value.

The Goodwill Perspective

This is what the helmet of salvation does for our prayer life and our life here on earth. We gain perspective on reality and relationships. When we look at our future salvation in Christ, the things of this world look very different. After adopting our daughters, Kim quit her job to become the CEO of our family. This cut in pay came with a lot of adjustments. One of the greatest adjustments has been our relationship with Goodwill. Kim and I used to be the people who bought new clothes at the mall and then gave them to Goodwill when we were tired of them. They usually were not worn out; we were just tired of looking at them. Now, we are the people who can't wait for half-price day at Goodwill. On the first Saturday of the month, we purchase slightly used clothing for a fraction of the cost we would pay at the mall. I'm disgusted when I go to a department store now and see a shirt for $75 that will be $2.75 at Goodwill. I can't stomach buying shoes—or anything, for that matter—at full price now that I see them through the eyes of a secondhand store.

Although our stock in clothing has fallen, our stock in relationships has grown. We are bullish on friendships and family. It's hard for me to sit in committee meetings on Tuesday nights knowing that there's a little girl who wants to play Chutes and Ladders at home. It doesn't matter that she changes the rules every time we play. I also hate being gone for bedtime. For the first 49 years of my life, I had no one to tuck into bed at night. For the first years of our daughter's lives, no one else could tuck them in. I'm determined to be the tucker-inner until the day that some rotten boy tears them out of our hands. Bedtime is when our family is the softest. All of the conflict of our day seems to fade away at bedtime as we snuggle in with prayers and hope for a better tomorrow. This is perspective. Perspective is what the helmet of salvation provides for us. Our future salvation in Christ devalues the things of this world and helps us to focus on the things that really matter. The person who takes up elements like the belt of truth and the breastplate of righteousness can't forget the perspective that comes from the helmet of salvation.

What Not to Wear

As we found with all of the other pieces in the armor of God, we have to lose something, in order for our helmet to fit. I have a box in my closet filled with hats. Each one is made with a specific function—whether I am protecting my head from the rays of the sun or from the gravel. The helmet of salvation, however, will not fit with any other headgear. It will never fit with our thickheaded FLM Syndrome! "First Let Me" Syndrome is found all over the Bible, and we suffer from it too. Jesus calls men to follow Him. A few of them say yes, but their response is "first, let me bury my father" or "first, let me say goodbye . . .

" Jesus expects us to discard any sense of self-reliance in order to trust Him with our salvation. I found salvation through Jesus when I finally admitted that I could not do it. I was not getting better on my own; no matter how hard I tried.

Jesus' disciple Peter struggled with the helmet of salvation because he was unwilling to lose his own self-reliance. "First, Let Me" seemed to be his first line of defense. He always had a better plan than God's plan and he would rather find a way to save himself instead of following someone else. Peter suffered from FLM Syndrome. We see this best when Jesus is washing the feet of His disciples. Peter lets Jesus know that there is no way in heaven or earth that he would ever allow Jesus to wash his feet. Peter would not allow it. He was a committed follower of Jesus. He would stand and fight for Jesus, but he struggled with surrender. Peter was a man's man who did not want anyone doing anything for him that he could do for himself. Having your feet washed demanded surrender. Peter's problem wasn't with dedication—he was a devoted follower. His problem was with surrender—with allowing Christ to do for him what he could never do for himself.

The Old Testament story of Hannah, on the other hand, is a beautiful picture of true surrender. After years of praying for a baby, Hannah makes a deal with God. She offers to surrender her child to the Lord's service if she could become pregnant. She does become pregnant and after weaning her son, Samuel, she takes him to the tabernacle in Shiloh. While others are dedicating their children, Hannah surrenders hers. She hands

Samuel over to Eli, the priest, and leaves. This is the picture of surrender. This is not just a picture of dedication; it's the picture of total trust. That is what Christ wants from His followers.

This is where Peter, and many of us, fall short. This is where Peter struggled the most because he wanted to remain dedicated to Jesus without actually surrendering to Him. Kyle Idleman, in his book *Not a Fan*, teaches that many of us are only fans of Jesus, but God wants so much more. Jesus lets Peter know that anything less than an unconditional surrender is unacceptable: "If I do not wash you, you have no part with Me" (John 13:8 NASB). Peter was continuing to follow Jesus, but refusing to join the team. He wanted the ability to save himself and he longed for the tools to change his own life, his own way.

This self-reliance, or FLM Syndrome, is incompatible with the helmet of salvation. Salvation comes from surrender. Salvation comes after we give up on our own attempts to change our lives. Salvation comes when we surrender to God's plan of salvation knowing that we cannot save ourselves. In some mysterious way, Jesus died on the cross to save us from the sins of our past. In some miraculous way, Jesus lives in us and saves us from the present. In some incredible way, we will be saved in the future, whether we are called out of this world at the sound of the trumpet or we slip from this world through the death of our bodies. We cannot accomplish this on our own and we cannot receive it if our response is, "first, let me."

Praying with the Helmet of Salvation

When we put on the helmet of salvation, we are constantly confessing our faith in Christ. We are reminding ourselves that our past is behind us and we are a new creation. Since this is a spiritual battle, we are reminding the forces of evil in the heavenly realms that we are safe. God saves us from our past, but He also has the power to save us physically in the present, much like the jailer in Philippi. We also gain perspective on our present reality by acknowledging our future resurrection. It would have been nice to begin with the helmet of salvation since this piece is so important to the rest of the armor. This understanding of salvation is extremely important for those who want to join forces against evil. The helmet is a reminder that God does not listen to our prayers because of our great communication skills. He listens because we are His children and we are safe in Him. We cannot gain the breastplate of righteousness on our own. We receive it from the one who purchased salvation for us. The readiness that comes from the gospel of peace is possible because of the ministry of reconciliation that Jesus brought to us and handed over for us to carry. Each piece of God's armor is a building block for the helmet of salvation. This changes everything about our present reality in heaven and on earth.

It's the helmet of salvation that allows us to pray some big, bold prayers. It's this understanding of salvation that gives us the faith to pray for physical as well as spiritual miracles. It's the helmet of salvation that helps us to know how to pray "in Jesus' name." After all, Jesus gave us carte blanche to pray in

His name. Whatever we agree on will be done. The perspective of our future salvation helps us to see those things that are inconsequential in light of our future hope. In light of our future hope, it's difficult for me to pray for a lot of material things in Jesus' name. Against the backdrop of salvation, it's hard for me to ask for selfish things that only advance my little kingdom. On the other hand, the experience of salvation gives me boldness to ask for my needs to be met in Christ. So this is how I pray using the helmet of salvation:

> Father, I thank You for saving me from my past and placing me into Your future. Protect me today from myself and from my enemies. Thank You for Your past, present, and future salvation, which is found in Jesus. Help me to see this life in light of Your salvation.

CHAPTER SEVEN

The Sword of the Spirit

"Take the . . . sword of the Spirit, which is the word of
God" (Ephesians 6:17).

In my spiritual battles, I've fallen deeply in love with the Bible.
Every time we went to Russia to try to bring our daughters home,
I had a scripture that helped me get through tough situations.
Forced to fly on some questionable airplanes to get to Siberia,
we were pretty nervous. Whenever the planes landed, everyone
on the plane would start clapping. I'm convinced that they were
celebrating surviving the flight. When I felt claustrophobic while
crammed into the back of a reconditioned cargo plane, or when
my seat came unbolted and I questioned the integrity of the
plane, I would quote 2 Timothy 1:7: "For God has not given us a
spirit of timidity, but of power and love and discipline" (NASB).
There were times when I was quoting the same scripture over
and over for hours at a time, but these powerful words calmed
my anxious spirit and allowed me to have perspective in some
very difficult times.

Alan Clark

As we were fighting for our children—and later, when we were watching my mom suffer with cancer—the Bible came alive for Kim and me. We were finding nuggets of wisdom and we held on to the promises of God. The sword of the Spirit is effective against the battles outside and inside of us. God's Word is an often neglected, yet strong weapon. We must remember that the Bible should be tempered by the other weapons in our arsenal. The Christian who has memorized large portions of the Bible still needs to wear the sandals of readiness in order to be gentle and respectful. The Word of God will be useless to the person who does not have the helmet of salvation in place. I tried to read the Bible my whole life and saw it as a boring history book until I met Jesus. After deciding to be a Christian, the Word of God became my story instead of history. I could see myself in so many of the Old Testament characters. I could also see my own temptations and shortcomings in the lives of the first disciples of Jesus. The sword of the Spirit is the perfect compliment to the armor of God and gives us identity, protection, and hope.

Trouble in Ephesus

In order to understand the purpose of this chapter, we need to dig a little deeper into the situation on the ground in Ephesus. The church in Ephesus was a church in turmoil. There were attitudes of superiority toward the Gentiles and there were prejudices on both sides of the aisle with Jews and Gentiles. Paul reminded these followers of Christ that the battles they were fighting were not battles against humans, but against the attitudes and prejudices of darkness that kept them from being brothers and sisters. The armor of God helped them break through these attitudes and prejudices. Paul had addressed the darkness that existed in homes, in marriages, in business, and in the church. This darkness was a spiritual battle and the armor of God was needed to fight the real battles of their day. Today, we fight the same battles. Marriages, families, and churches are split in two because Christians fight one another when they should be going into the battle together against the attitudes that bring isolation to our relationships. In order to be in step with God, we must be in step with one another against the real enemies that destroy homes and communities. In order to take back our homes and families we must take up the Word of God!

The last piece of armor that we are commanded to take up is the sword of the Spirit, which is the Word of God. This is the only offensive weapon in our arsenal. All of the other pieces of armor are meant to defend us from the enemy. The message was clear early on in the Bible. The devil and his evil forces lie in wait to ambush Christians. The belt of truth and the breastplate of righteousness are defensive weapons to show the enemy that he is already defeated and that we refuse to allow him to control our attitudes and thoughts. The other weapons in the armor are ones that define the battle and the boundaries of the battlefield. The sword of the Spirit is unique, but it must be joined together with the other pieces of our armor in order to rescue us from AWOL Christianity. We have been called to conquer and defeat these attitudes that cause isolation. After we put the enemy on high alert, we are able to go after the spiritual forces of darkness that have invaded God's territory.

A Weapon in Both Hands

The shield of faith and the sword of the Spirit are the two weapons with an explanation. We hold the shield in one hand and the sword in the other, so they go before us. *The shield extinguishes the words of the enemy and the sword is the Word of God.* The powerful hymn "A Mighty Fortress Is Our God" by Martin Luther expresses the power of the sword. In verse three, Luther writes:

> And though this world, with devils filled,
> Should threaten to undo us,
> We will not fear, for God hath willed
> His truth to triumph through us:
> The Prince of Darkness grim, we tremble not for him;
> His rage we can endure, for lo, his doom is sure,
> One little word shall fell him.

That last line is powerful. Luther knew the power of God's Word. It doesn't take the whole scripture to defeat the enemy. It doesn't even take a book of the Bible or a chapter. *The smallest words from God can defeat the biggest lies from the enemy!* Most Christians are embarrassed by their lack of Bible knowledge—feeling defeated and like failures when it comes to knowing the scriptures. Instead of standing on God's Word, we stand alone with the feeling of guilt because we do not know what others know. Some of us are afraid to speak the scriptures because we do not have a good understanding of the Bible and we are afraid that someone will trip us up with questions. Many of us have even tried to read the entire Bible, but at some point in the middle of February, we get bogged down in the book of Numbers and we give up.

A Word from God

Taking up the sword of the Spirit is not about having the entire Bible memorized. At some point in our walk, the Spirit of God will make a verse come to life. This verse will be tailored to fit the situation we are in and the Holy Spirit will highlight the meaning of this verse for our situation. When we began the adoption process, we realized that Kim would not be able to work when our daughters came home. Her job as a high school choral teacher demanded her attention from sun up to sun down on most days of the school year. During competition and musical seasons, Kim would leave the house at 7 a.m. and not get home until 8 p.m. for months at a time. We knew that this lifestyle was fun for a couple without children, but it would be detrimental to children who needed a mommy. Kim's income was often fifty percent of our total income during the year. We had been part of a DINK (Double Income No Kids) group in Dallas and we gave large amounts of money to every missionary and cause that came along. The Girl Scouts in our congregation knew that I would buy two boxes of cookies from every girl who asked us. We had boxes of thin mints for months.

At some point in our thirties, we learned to live debt free. Paying cash for cars and getting rid of thousands of dollars in credit card debt allowed us to, in the words of talk-show host Dave Ramsey, "live and give like no one else." So, in the middle of the adoption process, Kim quit her job to prepare for motherhood. We began looking at smaller homes and places to live that would be less expensive. We came up with a number of different scenarios and schemes that would help us to live with one car and to use electricity only on the weekends. On paper, we could not reconcile living on my salary alone. We went to a class on couponing and sold everything we could to put money in the bank. The adoption process was weighing us down and the large amounts of money we needed were taking chunks out of our bank account. We knew that we would need $10,000 in cash the next time we headed to Moscow. As Kim turned in her resignation letter to the school, we both began to worry about our future.

The enemy began to sow seeds of doubt in us. We had strong convictions about what these children would need when they came home, but our strong convictions were fighting the practical considerations of living, eating, saving for retirement, and providing for our family. As we sat in Sunday school one week, God opened Kim's eyes to Genesis 50:21: "So therefore, do not be afraid; I will provide for you and your little ones" (NASB). These were the words of Joseph to his brothers. The brothers were afraid that Joseph would treat them harshly, because they had been so mean to him. They were afraid that Joseph would use his power and influence in Egypt to punish them for the wounds they had inflicted upon him as a child. These were the words of Joseph, but the Holy Spirit touched Kim and let her know that the same promise that Joseph made to his brothers was God's promise to us. He would take care of our children and we would never have to worry about providing for them. As the Holy Spirit continued to confirm Kim's decision, she was reminded of the words of Jesus in Matthew 6 concerning God's provision in taking care of birds and flowers. He would care for our children and us.

In the coming months, our bills were overwhelming. We were bombarded with discouraging financial news as we lost $28,000 in a failed adoption attempt and had to start again with another agency. The enemy sent messages of doubt, failure, and fear, but Kim had a message from God. He would take care of our children. That's all she needed. We would sit at the table with a list of bills and fees, while she would quote God's promise. Genesis 50:21 was the word that she needed. She didn't need to quote a book of the Bible. When she was discouraged and filled with doubt, she would often just give the reference and we would dig out of the darkness. This is the sword of the Spirit. This is the offensive weapon that pierces through fear and doubt.

Once again we are reminded that the battle is the Lord's. Provision for our needs is God's job. We are called to get in step with Him. Once we claimed this promise, we realized that God had already provided for our needs. In the late 1960s, my grandmother worked for a clothing store in New Orleans. She was in charge of depositing money in the bank every evening. With tremendous foresight, every night she would take out all of the real silver coins and replace them with her own dollar bills. Alloys were replacing the silver coins of the 60s and she believed that these coins would be valuable someday. My dad had been telling me for 20 years that he had a box in his bank vault from my grandmother, but I knew it was just a bunch of silly coins and I had no interest in them.

As God was teaching us how to live on one salary, the Holy Spirit reminded me that there was a box in dad's bank vault. One afternoon, as we were scraping money together to go to Moscow, my dad brought the box to me. It had never been opened and I knew my late grandmother's handwriting on the box as soon as I saw it. She had scribbled "Only for Alan Michael Clark" on an envelope and placed it on the box. The box was very heavy. When I opened it I saw beautiful silver dimes and half dollars arranged neatly and stacked orderly by a very caring hand. My mouth dropped open when a coin dealer told me that this box of coins was worth thousands of dollars. God once again reminded us of His promise to care for us. Imagine a little old lady in New Orleans, Louisiana, in 1968 walking to the bank, guided by an unseen hand to put silver coins in a box. If that doesn't give you chills thinking about God's foreknowledge and provision, I don't know what will.

Kim and I often stress about our bills. Now that we have children, our medical bills in one month have been as high as $2,500 after some dental work and an emergency visit to the ER. Yet, God continues to provide for us and for our children. The enemy would like to convince us that we're going to run out of money and we'll be broke in retirement. God continues to provide for us and we continue to stand on the Word that He gave us. An unexpected envelope arrived in the mail with money to start a college fund for each of our children. An unexpected gift allowed us to have a new car. We face huge bills every month, and God's provides for us. At times, He provides through our work and at times He provides through His grace.

Through personal Bible study, discipleship lessons, and sermons, God will highlight a verse to give you a word of encouragement. He'll provide the words that you need to fight the battles that He has called you to fight. As we are called to fight with God against the spiritual forces of evil in the heavenly realms, He provides the weapons that we need.

What Not to Wear

The sword of the Spirit is incompatible with other weapons we might want to use. We only have two hands with which to hold the shield of faith and the sword of the Spirit. We cannot hold on to other weapons that compromise our use of the sword—the Word of God. The bomb of wishful thinking is useless against the enemy. A Nashville news anchor recently ended his report by letting some victims know that we would cross our fingers and pray for them. Crossing our fingers is useless—never mind the fact that it would be a very uncomfortable way to hold a sword. Many friends will ask you to send them good thoughts and some people will tell us they are thinking about us during hard times. This does nothing for us other than help us to feel better. Good thoughts will not erase prejudice and fix isolation in relationships. Good thoughts will not fix churches, marriages, families, or communities. The enemy in the spiritual realms is not afraid of your good thoughts, no matter how good they might be. *The presence of dopamine in my brain may increase, but it has no effect on the greed, prejudice, and evil in my heart.* If we are going to stand with God against the forces that split relationships, we are going to have to do the work of a prayer warrior. It may be more convenient to spend our day thinking good thoughts for our friends that are hurting, but we must, instead, storm the gates of heaven and ask God to move mountains.

In order to enjoy the victory that is ours, we must replace our good thoughts with God's Word. Praying Scripture is mountain-moving prayer. Standing on God's promises for provision and protection will see amazing results that will not come from positive thinking. Instead of trying to send positive energy to a friend in need, pray Psalm 121 over them, "I lift up my eyes to the hills—from where will my help come? My help comes from the LORD, who made heaven and earth" (121:1–2 NRSV). When we enter into God's battles, it's best to use God's weapons. Remember the words of Martin Luther, "One little word will fell him." When praying for your family, it's best to put a scripture next to the name of every child. This is done over time and is not just an exercise of the mind. Pray for your children and ask the Lord to give you a verse to help guide them. We have three daughters, so we have verses that apply to each of them. These verses change over time, but I believe that God will give us the promises we need as we navigate through the teen years and into adulthood with them. Sending positive thoughts their way will give me a temporary boost, but I can get the same energy from those Girl Scout cookies.

No More Kittens

When Kim and I married, we received a dozen or so pillows, pictures, plates, and other items with quotes or sayings on them. They were sayings about marriage, friendship, and the joy of relationships. My mother-in-law had Isaiah 33:6 printed and framed for me as a gift: "He will be the sure foundation for your times, a rich store of salvation and wisdom and knowledge; the fear of the LORD is the key to this treasure." This verse was her prayer for me. She let me know that she stood on this verse for me when she prayed for me. In the ministry, I've had a number of difficult times where I felt alone. A picture of a cat with the words "hang in there" does not help me when friends walk away. A wise saying on a picture of a lighthouse has never pulled me through the turmoil that comes when I feel threatened. When I struggle, I look up from my desk and see the verse that Sue gave to me 30 years ago. I don't try to think good thoughts when my world crumbles. I simply thank God for being my stability when the world around me is failing. I often thank Him for being my portion. As a minister of the gospel I get an extra serving of grace, because I'm required to share it so freely. I'm glad that my mother-in-law did not give me a frame about good thoughts and puppies. Instead, she gave me a sword that has defeated despair on many occasions. Stop settling for good thoughts, and pick up the sword of the Spirit—the Word of God!

Putting on the armor of God will make you a game changer in your church and family. You'll be able to stand against the enemies of bad attitudes, greed, and prejudice. You'll be able to help other soldiers understand their identity in Christ and to stand against the enemy. The sword of the Spirit—the final piece of the armor—should be held with respect. We should never take it lightly. Open up your Bible and begin to see your life in God's story. Find a verse to hold on to. You will be surprised at the power you possess by standing on the promises of God!

CHAPTER EIGHT

On Your Mark, Get Set, PRAY

In these chapters, we uncovered some amazing truths about the armor of God. Understanding these truths brought stability to our lives as we went through the adoption process. In June of 2012, we finally brought our children home from Siberia. The two-year ordeal left us worn out. As the children settled into life here in the US, my mom continued her battle with cancer. She lost the battle in July of 2013. We are thankful that our children had the chance to meet her. We are also thankful that they experienced a real grandma who would move heaven and earth to make sure they had cookies.

As I've gone through days of doubts and struggle, I've been able to stand against the enemy by putting on the full armor of God each morning. The belt of truth alone can consume a large portion of my prayers. I know that God loves me and that He has a plan for each of our children. I know that God can hear me. He sees me when I struggle. I know that He is present in our lives at all times and in all places. After going over the truths that I know, I move through the pieces of armor and I carefully put on each item. Some of these items help me to understand my identity in Christ. As I put on the breastplate of righteousness, I'm reminded that I am a child of God. As I put on the sandals of readiness, I am reminded of my calling to be a peacemaker. As I am dressed in each item of God's armor, my trust and faith begins to grow. By the time I begin to quote scriptures and take up the Word of God, I can almost see the devil running from our house and our church.

We've learned how to stand like conquerors. We've learned how to let the spiritual forces of evil know that they are not welcome in our homes, churches, and communities. We've learned how to proclaim our freedom, faith, and position with God in order to establish authority against evil. Paul taught the church in Ephesus that the enemy is not the Jew or Gentile who looks, smells, and thinks differently than you. The enemy is not your spouse, or even your employer. Your enemies are the attitudes, prejudices, and other forces coming from an evil realm—a realm that is real and powerful. In order to fight these enemies, we must put on God's armor and not our own. We must be fitted to fight the good fight with God's armor and God's weapons.

Conclusion

I would like to conclude this book with ways to use the armor of God in prayer. There are times when the armor of God can serve as a warm-up for prayer. It is like stretching before working out.

It helps me to get focused and serious. As I go through each piece of the armor I often picture myself putting on a suit of armor. I simply go through each item before praying. Here is a sample of this kind of warm up:

Father, I put on the belt of truth. I am fitted with the breastplate of Your righteousness. My feet are fitted with the readiness that comes from the gospel of peace. I take up the shield of faith and the helmet of salvation. I'm taking up Your Word in order to have your full armor covering me today as I begin to pray.

This simple opening is an amazing way to begin our prayers. It puts our enemies on high alert and moves mountains. We can also use the armor of God as an outline for praying. Here is a sample of my daily prayers and the way that I work through God's armor in this way:

The Belt of Truth

Father, I thank You that You hear me this morning. I put on the belt of truth, knowing that You hear me. I know that You see me. I know that You love me. I wear the belt of a champion because I know that Jesus has conquered my enemies. I know that You love our children. I know that You are watching over Kim and the girls today. I know that the church is in Your hands.

The Breastplate of Righteousness

I thank You that I'm welcome in Your presence because Jesus has placed the breastplate of righteousness on me. I come into Your presence without guilt, because the blood of Jesus is stronger than my past failures. Being a follower of Jesus makes me Your child and gives me access to an intimate walk with You. Thank You for giving me rights in Your Kingdom.

The Sandals of Readiness

I'll join You today in bringing peace to situations. My shoes are prepared to walk over turmoil with peace. I desire to be a peacemaker today and hope others will see me as a Your child. Help me to stomp out fires and to perform the ministry of reconciliation. Help me to reconcile people to You and to one another.

The Shield of Faith

I'm covered by Your shield, knowing that You reward those who earnestly seek You. I look for Your blessings today, knowing that You are looking to strengthen those who are committed to You. My eyes are open to see where You are working in my life and in the situations that I will face today.

The Helmet of Salvation

Thank You for the helmet of salvation on my head. I'm saved from my past sin. I confess that You are able to keep me from stumbling in the present. My future is secure in Your hands. I will see the world in view of these eternal truths today.

The Sword of the Spirit

Thank You for Kim, and I pray that You will be her portion and shield this morning. As our children go to school today, we are reminded that bad company corrupts good morals. We trust that You will help our children to find good company today. I pray for the church today, knowing that the gates of hell cannot stand against us.

The sword of the Spirit will take up the majority of my prayers as I pray for the people and situations in our lives and assign a scripture to each of them.

Stand

May God bless you as you use the armor of God as a guide for prayer or as preparation for praying. Churches that teach these principles do not need to be afraid of the enemy that can tear their fellowships apart. The enemies of God will run from the congregation that will stand their ground. The apostle Paul commanded the church in Ephesus to stand. They were obviously fearful of standing up to the enemies of God. Paul was tired of seeing the church defeated when they had massive weapons of destruction at their disposal. We need to rediscover these weapons and learn how to stand in the 21st century.

Don't forget to put on the full armor of God. If we put on the belt of truth but we forget to put on the helmet of salvation, we lose our perspective and the enemy will see a chink in the armor. If we proudly wear the helmet of salvation and forget the belt of truth, we will misunderstand salvation and the enemy will see a chink in the armor. The Christian who is fitted from head to toe will be able to stand against the enemy and stand for Christ.

Made in the
USA
Middletown, DE